PRACTICE QUESTIONS for HIGHER PHYSICS

Campbell Robertson

Selected problems for the Scottish Higher Physics course

- complements NQ **Complete Higher Physics Revision Notes**
- ideal for revision and exam preparation
- over 300 extended and short answer questions
- coverage of the whole of the Higher Physics syllabus
- questions designed to suit all levels of ability
- all numerical answers included

Preface

One of the key elements to achieving success at Higher Physics is to ensure adequate practice in questions of the right type. Students of Higher Physics can usually achieve this by attempting questions from Physics past papers but unfortunately this route has its drawbacks. The student may not really be ready to tackle the harder problem-solving aspects found in many Higher questions and may not get the opportunity to try questions which cover the whole course.

The aim of this book is to try to overcome these problems and its content covers the Higher syllabus very closely. Questions have been set which examine all the learning outcomes as laid down by the Scottish Qualifications Authority. The questions have been structured to give a natural progression from relatively simple problems to those which require a certain degree of skill in problem solving. It is hoped that you, the student, will be able to progress from one to the other in manageable steps as you work through the questions.

Questions are of a mixture of types. Some relate directly to the use of formulae and these have been presented in table form. This should provide opportunity to re-arrange formulae and establish that you are carrying out the basics correctly. Apart from a few short questions, most are longer and are similar to those which will be met in the final NQ Higher exam.

Campbell Robertson

Published by
P&N Publications
1 Wallace Street
Bannockburn
Stirling
FK7 8JQ

COPYING PROHIBITED

NOTE: This publication is NOT licensed for copying under the Copyright Licensing Agency's Scheme.
All rights reserved. No part of this publication may be reproduced, stored in a retrieval system or transmitted in any form by any means—electric, mechanical, photocopying or otherwise—without prior permission of the publisher P&N Publications, 1 Wallace Street, Bannockburn, Stirling FK7 8JQ.

© P&N Publications

CONTENTS

UNIT 1 Mechanics and Properties of Matter

Vectors
Vectors and scalars   1

Equations of Motion
Graphs of motion   5
The equations of motion   6
Acceleration due to gravity – vertical motion   8
Horizontal projectiles   9
Projectiles at an angle   10

Newton's Second Law, Energy and Power
Newton's Second Law   13

Momentum and Impulse
Momentum   19
Impulse   22

Density and Pressure
Density of gases, liquids and solids   24
Pressure, force and area   26
Buoyancy   27

The Gas Laws
Pressure and volume   28
Pressure and temperature   30
Volume and temperature   32
The General Gas Equation   29

UNIT 2 Electricity and Electronics

Electric Fields and Resistors in Circuits
Electric fields   35
E.m.f. and internal resistance   36
Resistors in circuits   41
Wheatstone Bridge   45

Alternating Current and Voltage
Alternating current   51

Capacitance
Charge, voltage and capacitance   52
Energy stored on a capacitor   54
Charging and discharging capacitors   56
Capacitors and a.c.   57
Applications of capacitors   58

Analogue Electronics
Inverting amplifiers   60
Differential amplifiers   64

UNIT 3 Radiation and Matter

Waves
Wave characteristics	69
Interference	69
Diffraction gratings	74

Refraction of Light
Refractive index of light	76
Total internal reflection	79

Optoelectronics and Semiconductors
Intensity of radiation	82
Photoelectric emission	84
Emission and absorption spectra	86
Lasers	89
Semiconductors	90

Nuclear Reactions
Nature of radiation	94
Fission and fusion	96

Dosimetry and Safety
Absorbed dose, dose equivalent and effective dose equivalent	97
Gamma ray absorption	99

Uncertainties 101

APPENDIX (i) Higher Formulae 105

APPENDIX (ii) Units, Prefixes and Scientific Notation 111

APPENDIX (iii) Data sheet 112

APPENDIX (iv) Answers to Numerical Problems 113

UNIT 1 Mechanics and Properties of Matter

Vectors

Vectors and scalars

1.1 (*a*) Define what is meant by a scalar quantity.

  (*b*) Define what is meant by a vector quantity.

  (*c*) Separate the following list into vector and scalar quantities:

  (i) speed
  (ii) distance
  (iii) acceleration
  (iv) velocity
  (v) temperature
  (vi) mass
  (vii) displacement
  (viii) force
  (ix) weight
  (x) energy

1.2 During athletics training a runner sprints along a straight track for a distance of 115 m in a time of 13 s. He then turns around and jogs back towards the starting line for a distance of 25 m. This takes a further 7 s.

  (*a*) (i) What is the total **distance** travelled by the runner?

   (ii) Find the runner's average **speed**.

  (*b*) (i) What is the total **displacement** of the runner?

   (ii) Find his average **velocity**.

  (*c*) (i) What would be the runner's displacement if he was to return to the starting point of his sprint?

   (ii) What would this make his average velocity?

1.3 During an orienteering competition a competitor travels a distance of 300 m due east followed by 800 m due north as shown below.

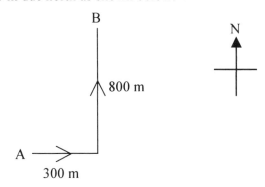

  (*a*) What is the total displacement of the competitor having moved from A to B? (Remember that vectors have direction as well as magnitude.)

  (*b*) Orienteers use a system of 3 figure bearings e.g. due north has bearing 000°, due east is 090° and so on. What would have been the bearing of the orienteer if she had travelled 800 m east instead of 300 m?

1.4 Find the resultant vector for the following combination of vectors by drawing a scale diagram.

(a) Displacements.

(i)
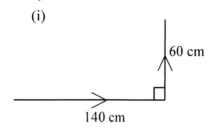

(ii)
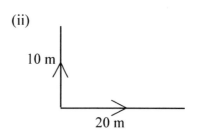

(iii)
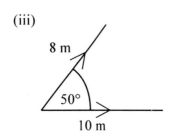

(iv)
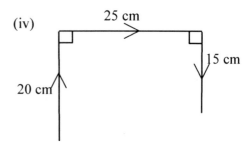

(b) Velocities.

(i)
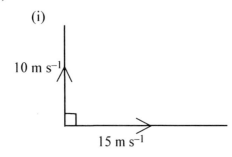

(ii)
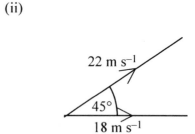

(iii)
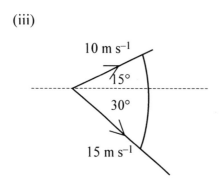

(iv)
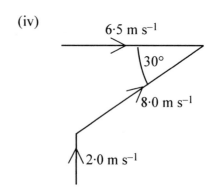

1.5 Find the magnitude of the rectangular components of the following vectors.

(a)
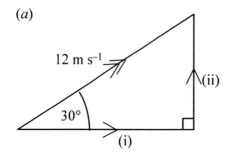

(b)
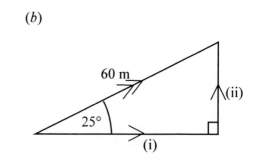

1.6 A ferry has to cross a stretch of water but the tide is flowing at right angles to its intended path. If the current is flowing at 5 m s⁻¹ east and the ferry travels at 3 m s⁻¹ north, find the resultant velocity if it travels from A to B.

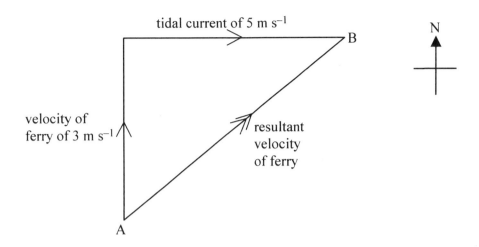

1.7 A robot arm in a factory moves a component forwards a distance of 1·5 m and then to the right a distance of 2·3 m.

Draw a scale diagram to show what single displacement could be used to replace these two movements.

1.8 A bird is flying due south with a velocity of 3 m s⁻¹. Find the resultant velocity of the bird if it experiences a head wind of 2 m s⁻¹, 30° west of north.

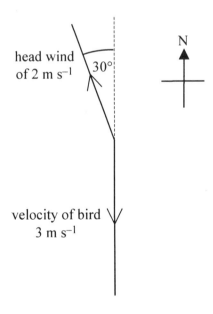

1.9 (*a*) An aeroplane is flying at a speed of 130 m s^{-1} m at an angle of 15° above the horizontal. Find:

  (i) the horizontal component;

  (ii) the vertical component of this flight velocity.

(*b*) During its flight the aeroplane flies at a bearing of 000° due north for 140 km. It then turns north-east at a bearing of 040° and flies a distance of 100 km before turning east at a bearing of 080° and flying on this course for 60 km.

  (i) Find the total distance the flight covered.

  (ii) What was the resultant displacement of the flight?

  (iii) Find the velocity of the plane if it covered this section of flight in a time of 40 minutes.

(*c*) What would have been the resultant velocity of the plane had there been a headwind acting due south (180°) with a velocity of 20 m s^{-1}?

1.10 During its launch a shuttle is flying with a velocity of 1200 m s^{-1}. The vertical component of this velocity is 600 m s^{-1}.

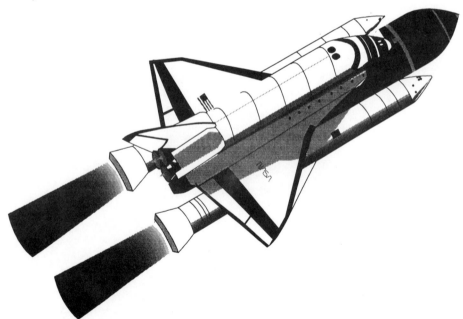

(*a*) (i) Find the horizontal component of the shuttle's velocity.

  (ii) If the shuttle maintains the same velocity of 1200 m s^{-1} but decreases its angle of flight, what change will take place in the magnitude of its horizontal component?

(*b*) The acceleration of the shuttle is 24 m s^{-2} at an angle of 30° above the horizontal. If the value of acceleration due to gravity is 9·8 m s^{-2} vertically downwards, what will be the resultant acceleration of the shuttle?

Equations of Motion

Graphs of motion

1.11 Look at the three velocity-time graphs shown below. Sketch the equivalent acceleration-time graph for each motion.

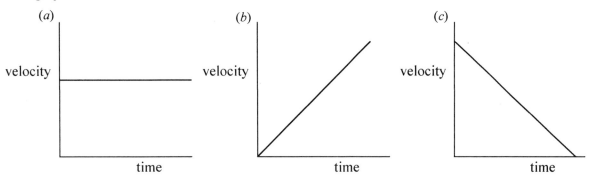

1.12 Look at the velocity-time graph for the motion of ball which has been thrown straight up into the air then allowed to fall to the ground.

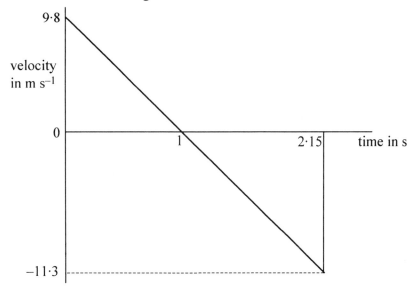

(a) Explain why the graph has sections above the horizontal axis and below the horizontal axis.

(b) Describe the nature of the acceleration of the ball during its flight.

(c) Using information from the graph, calculate the acceleration of the ball.

(d) (i) Calculate the height to which the ball rises.

(ii) What vertical distance did the ball fall?

(iii) Using information from parts (i) and (ii) of this question, find the height above the ground from which the ball was thrown upwards.

(e) Describe a way in which the acceleration of the ball could be measured experimentally. Include in your answer:

(i) a list of the apparatus required;

(ii) details of how the experiment would be carried out;

(iii) an explanation of how the results would be used to find the acceleration of the ball.

1.13 The **velocity-time** graph below was produced by a ball which was thrown into the air before falling and bouncing several times.

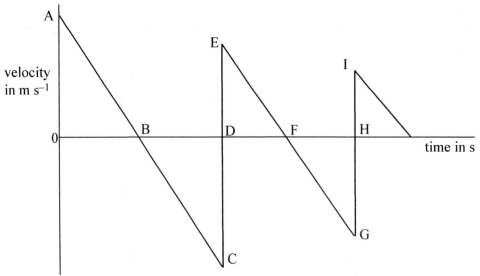

(a) At which point on the graph, represented by the letters A to I, did the ball **first** strike the floor?

(b) Sketch an **acceleration-time** graph for the motion of the ball between A and C.

(c) The area under the graph between A and B is more than the area under the line between E and F. Explain this difference.

The equations of motion

1.14 Look at the graph below produced by a vehicle which starts at an initial velocity, u, then accelerates to a final velocity, v in a time of t seconds.

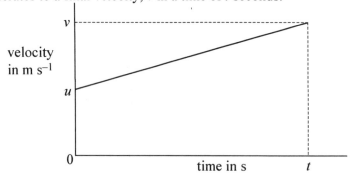

Show how the graph can be used to derive the equation $s = ut + \frac{1}{2}at^2$.

1.15 Use the formula $v = u + at$ to find the missing entries in the following table.

	Initial velocity	Final velocity	Acceleration	Time
(a)	0 m s^{-1}	60 m s^{-1}	3 m s^{-2}	
(b)	8 m s^{-1}		2 m s^{-2}	4 s
(c)	10 m s^{-1}	20 m s^{-1}		5 s
(d)		8 m s^{-1}	0·5 m s^{-2}	6 s

© P&N Publications

1.16 Use the formula $v^2 = u^2 + 2as$ to find the missing entries in the following table.

	Initial velocity	Final velocity	Acceleration	Displacement
(a)	0 m s⁻¹	20 m s⁻¹		80 m
(b)	200 m s⁻¹	800 m s⁻¹	4 m s⁻²	
(c)	0 m s⁻¹		0·2 m s⁻²	8 m
(d)		25 m s⁻¹	5 m s⁻²	22·5 m

1.17 Use the formula $s = ut + \frac{1}{2}at^2$ to find the missing entries in the following table.

	Displacement	Initial velocity	Time	Acceleration
(a)		0 m s⁻¹	5 s	10 m s⁻²
(b)	100 m		2 s	10 m s⁻²
(c)	75 m	0 m s⁻¹		1·25 m s⁻²
(d)	5 m	0·5 m s⁻¹	0·2 s	

1.18 A cyclist accelerates at 1·5 m s⁻² for 4 seconds. If her final speed is 14 m s⁻¹ find her initial speed.

1.19 A train is approaching a station at 4 m s⁻¹ when its brakes are applied. 10 s later it has covered a distance of 20 m. Find the deceleration of the train.

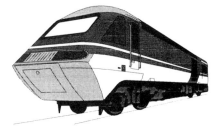

1.20 A boy cycles at 6 m s⁻¹ then jams on his brakes and skids to rest in a distance of 4·5 m. Calculate the deceleration of the cyclist and his bicycle.

1.21 A jumbo jet has to reach a speed of 100 m s⁻¹ in order to be able to take off successfully. What will be the minimum acceleration required if the runway available has a length of 1800 m?

1.22 A car accelerates from a stationary start to a speed of 25 m s⁻¹ in a time of 15 s. Find the distance travelled by the car in that time.

1.23 An air rifle pellet accelerates from rest to 100 m s⁻¹ whilst travelling down the barrel of the air rifle. If the barrel of the rifle is 0·6 m long, find the acceleration of the pellet.

Acceleration due to gravity–vertical motion

NOTE: In problems 24 to 39 the value used for acceleration due to gravity is $g = 9.8$ m s^{-2}.

1.24 A stone is dropped down a deep well. A splash is heard when the stone hits the water 2·5 s later. Calculate the depth of the well.

1.25 A drip falls from a leaking tap and hits the ground with a speed of 4 m s^{-1}. How far above the ground was the drip when it fell from the end of the tap?

1.26 A ball is thrown vertically into the air with a velocity of 14 m s^{-1}.

   (*a*) State the velocity of the ball when at its maximum height.

   (*b*) Calculate the height the ball reaches.

   (*c*) State the velocity with which the ball will return to its starting position.

   (*d*) Calculate the total time for the flight of the ball.

1.27 A helicopter is flying vertically **upwards** with a velocity of 4 m s^{-1} when it releases a package of medical supplies to an aid team.

   (*a*) Describe the motion of the package from the instant it is released.

   (*b*) Calculate the height from which the package was dropped if it hits the ground 3 s after being released.

   (*c*) Calculate the final velocity of the package when it hits the ground.

1.28 A ball is thrown upwards at 15 m s^{-1}.

   (*a*) How long will it take to reach its maximum height?

   (*b*) What will be the maximum height it reaches?

   (*c*) Find the height of the ball above the ground when it is travelling downwards at 8 m s^{-1}.

1.29 An arrow is shot vertically into the air with a velocity of 60 m s^{-1}.

   (*a*) Find the expected time it would take for the arrow to return to its starting position if it went vertically up and then returned vertically back down to earth?

   (*b*) What height would the arrow have reached?

   (*c*) In practice, the time to reach maximum height is different from that calculated. State in what way it is different, giving a reason for your answer, and the effect this has on the height the arrow reaches.

Horizontal projectiles

1.30 An air rifle is pointed horizontally and a pellet fired with a velocity of 100 m s^{-1}.

(a) (i) Describe the horizontal motion of the pellet.

(ii) Describe the vertical motion of the pellet.

(b) (i) What will be the **initial vertical velocity** of the pellet?

(ii) Calculate the final vertical velocity of the pellet if it was fired from a height of 1·8 m above the ground.

(c) By scale drawing or other means, find the resultant velocity of the pellet when it hits the ground.

1.31 During a volleyball match the volleyball is pushed horizontally over the net with a velocity of 6 m s^{-1}.

(a) How long will it take the ball to reach the ground if the height from which it was released was 2 m?

(b) How far behind the net will the ball strike the ground?

(c) Find the resultant velocity of the ball when it strikes the ground (i.e. its combined horizontal and vertical velocity).

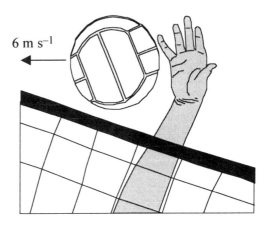

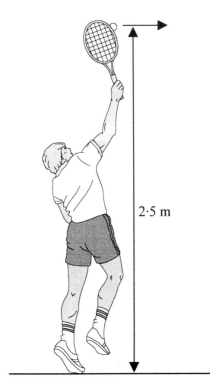

1.32 A player returns a tennis ball by striking it horizontally at a height of 2·5 m above the ground. The ball crosses over the net and bounces on the ground a distance of 12 m from the player.

(a) Calculate the final vertical velocity of the ball just before it strikes the ground.

(b) Calculate the time it takes for the ball to reach the point where it bounces.

(c) What was the initial horizontal velocity of the ball when it was struck by the racquet?

© P&N Publications

Projectiles at an angle

1.33 A shell is projected at an angle of 60° above the horizontal with a velocity of 230 m s^{-1}.

   (a) Calculate the vertical velocity of the shell.

   (b) Calculate the horizontal velocity of the shell.

1.34 A projectile is fired with a velocity of 25 m s^{-1} at an angle of 30° above the horizontal. Any effect due to air resistance can be ignored.

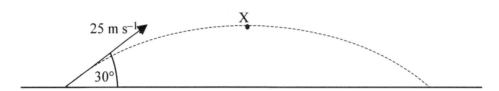

   (a) Calculate:

   (i) the initial vertical component of the projectile's velocity;

   (ii) the initial horizontal component of the projectile's velocity.

   (b) (i) What will be the vertical component of the projectile's velocity when at maximum height at point X?

   (ii) What will be the horizontal component of the projectile's velocity when at maximum height at point X?

   (c) Calculate the maximum height reached by the projectile.

   (d) Calculate the time taken for:

   (i) the projectile to reach its maximum height;

   (ii) the time taken for the total flight.

1.35 A footballer kicks a stationary ball and it leaves his foot with a velocity of 14 m s^{-1} at an angle of 20° above the horizontal.

   (a) Calculate:

   (i) the horizontal component of the ball's velocity;

   (ii) the vertical component of the ball's velocity.

   (b) Find the time taken for the ball to reach its maximum height.

   (c) What was the total time for the flight of the ball?

   (d) How far did the ball land from where it was kicked?

1.36 An experiment is carried out on projectiles within an aeroplane flying at high altitude. The graphs below were obtained during one of the experiments and show the components of velocity of a projectile.

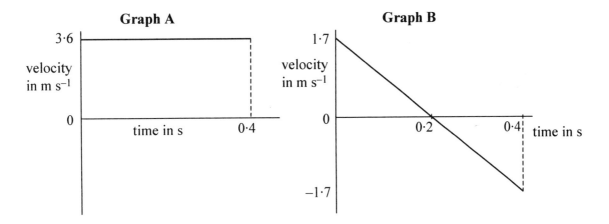

(a) State which graph represents the horizontal motion of the projectile and which the vertical motion.

(b) What effect will the high altitude have on the value of gravitational field strength?

(c) Use the graphs to obtain a value for the acceleration due to gravity.

(d) Find the height the projectile reaches.

(e) Find the range of the projectile.

(f) By means of a scale drawing or otherwise, find the velocity at which the projectile was fired.

1.37 A motorcyclist is attempting to jump across a gap which requires that his bike should travel at least 8 m without dropping below the level of the takeoff ramp. The end of the ramp is at an angle of 25°. Initially the takeoff ramp and landing site are level with each-other.

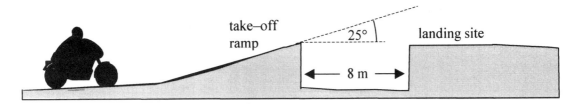

(a) (i) What will be the minimum horizontal component of his velocity if he crosses the 8 m gap in a time of 0·3 s?

(ii) Calculate the resultant takeoff velocity of the motorcyclist.

(b) To make it easier, the height of the landing site is lowered so that it is 1 m lower than the end of the takeoff ramp. What effect will this have on the necessary takeoff speed of the motorcyclist? Explain your answer.

© P&N Publications

1.38 A ball is allowed to roll down a ramp to the edge of a table as shown below and hits the ground 0·4 s later.

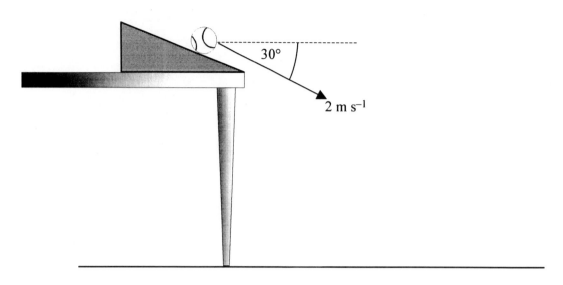

(a) How high is the table?

(b) What will be the horizontal distance between the edge of the table and the position on the floor where the ball lands?

1.39 A golf ball is struck and rises into the air with a velocity of 15 m s^{-1}. It reaches its maximum height after 1·25 s.

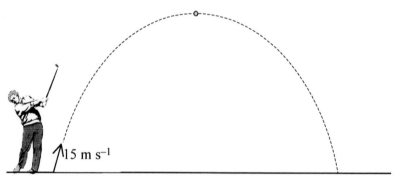

(a) Calculate:

    (i) the initial vertical velocity of the golf ball;

    (ii) the initial horizontal velocity of the golf ball.

(b) How far from the golfer did the ball land?

Newton's Second Law, Energy and Power

Newton's Second Law

1.40 A car engine is capable of providing a force of 2000 N at its wheels. Find the acceleration of the car if it has a mass of 800 kg. Ignore the effect of friction.

1.41 A popular attraction in amusement arcades is a table version of ice hockey where a plastic disc called a puck rides on a cushion of air. This is pushed using a hand-held 'stick'. The mass of the stick is 0·3 kg and the puck has a mass of 0·05 kg. Assume there is no friction present.

(a) When initially pushed the puck is in contact with the stick. Find the acceleration of the puck if a force of 1·75 N is applied to the stick.

(b) Describe the motion of the puck when it is no longer in contact with the stick.

1.42 Two boxes are tied together by a string. A second string is used to apply a force to the boxes as shown in the diagram below. Assume there are no frictional forces acting.

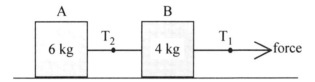

(a) What is the tension in the string at point T_1 if the boxes accelerate at 3 m s^{-2}?

(b) What will be the tension in the string at point T_2?

(c) The boxes are now pulled onto a surface where there is a frictional force of 5 N acting on each box. What must be the tension in the string at T_1 to maintain an acceleration of 3 m s^{-2}?

1.43 A balloon is floating above the ground. The total mass of the balloon and its passengers is 320 kg.

(a) What is the weight of the balloon?

(b) What will be the minimum buoyancy force which the balloon can provide if it is to just float in a stationary position?

(c) By turning on the gas burner to produce more hot air the buoyancy force **increases** by 44 N. The balloonist also releases ballast in the form of sand. As a result of these changes the mass of the balloon falls to 310 kg. What will be the acceleration of the balloon?

1.44 A crane is raising a load of timber with a mass of 280 kg. When first being raised from the ground the timber has an acceleration of 0·2 m s⁻².

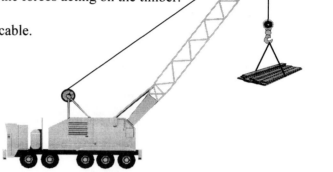

(a) Draw a diagram to show all the forces acting on the timber.

(b) Calculate the tension in the cable.

(c) What will be the tension in the cable when the timber is being raised at a steady speed?

1.45 A parachutist is descending at a steady speed of 12 m s⁻¹. The mass of the parachutist and her parachute is 70 kg. As she descends she experiences a side wind which generates a steady horizontal force of 20 N on her from left to right.

(a) Draw a diagram showing the direction and magnitude of all the forces acting on her.

(b) By pulling cords attached to her parachute she is able to control its rate of descent. As a result she begins to accelerate downwards at 0·5 m s⁻².

   (i) Calculate the unbalanced force acting on her vertically downwards.

   (ii) By scale drawing, find the resultant force acting on her at this point in time.

1.46 A fireworks rocket has a total mass of 1·5 kg. When it is fired it produces a total thrust of 90 N.

(a) What is the weight of the rocket just after it is launched?

(b) Find the initial acceleration of the rocket.

(c) The graph below represents the velocity of the rocket during its journey to maximum height.

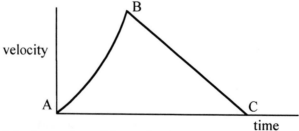

Describe and explain the motion of the rocket between:

   (i) A and B;

   (ii) B and C.

1.47 A science teacher with a mass of 70 kg stands in a school lift travelling from the ground floor to the second floor of the school. As part of an experiment he stands on a set of bathroom scales in order to measure his weight.

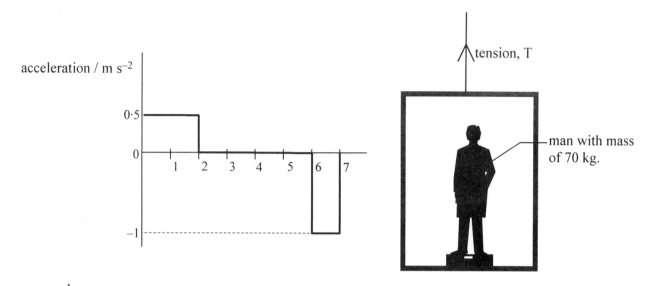

(a) What would the scales read when the lift was at rest?

(b) The lift now undergoes the motion shown in the graph above. What would the bathroom scales read between:

(i) 0 to 2 seconds;

(ii) 2 to 6 seconds;

(iii) 6 to 7 seconds?

(c) If the lift has a total mass of 1200 kg, including the teacher, what must be the tension in the cable supporting the lift between:

(i) 0 to 2 seconds;

(ii) 2 to 6 seconds;

(iii) 6 to 7 seconds?

1.48 A pupil with a mass of 45 kg stands on a set of bathroom scales in a lift. The bathroom scales read 351 N.

(a) Find the unbalanced force acting on the pupil.

(b) Describe the motion of the lift if it were going downwards at the time.

1.49 Find the resultant force acting on the masses below and hence find their resultant acceleration.

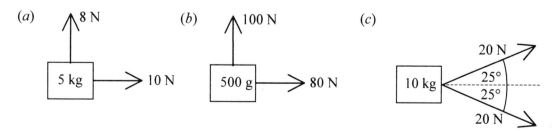

1.50 A very old tree is in danger of falling down whenever there is a strong wind. To prevent this it is supported by a guy-rope as shown below.

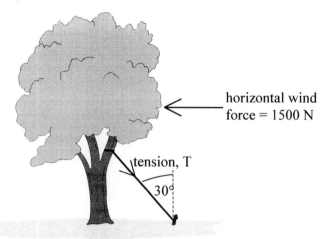

Calculate the value of tension in the rope when it just balances a horizontal wind force of 1500 N.

1.51 A set of six slotted masses with a total mass of 0·6 kg are suspended from a piece of stretched elastic.

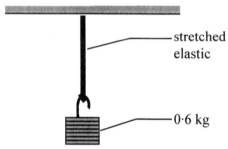

The slotted masses are initially at rest. Calculate the initial upward acceleration of those remaining when one 0·1 kg mass is removed.

1.52 A box rests on an inclined slope as shown below.

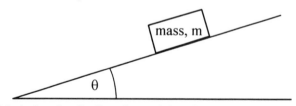

Complete the table below by finding the weight of the box and hence the components of its weight acting parallel with and perpendicular to the slope.

	Mass, m	Weight of box	Angle θ	Component of weight parallel with slope	Component of weight perpendicular to slope
(a)	2 kg		30°		
(b)	10 kg		20°		
(c)	250 g		30°		
(d)	1 kg		45°		

© P&N Publications

1.53 A trolley with a mass of 8 kg is stationary on a slope at an angle of 15°.

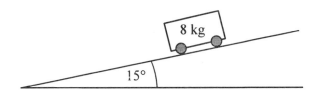

  (a) What is the component of the trolley's weight which is acting parallel with the slope?

  (b) What must be the value of the friction acting against the trolley?

1.54 A skier with a mass of 65 kg skis down a slope of 20°. His acceleration down the slope is 0·5 m s^{-2}. Calculate the value of friction acting against him.

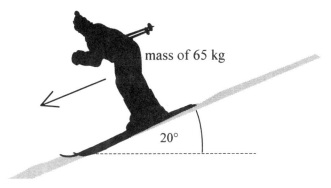

1.55 A car with a mass of 850 kg freewheels down a slope with an acceleration of 0·45 m s^{-2}. The slope is at an angle of 20° to the horizontal.

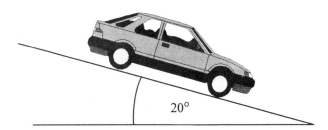

  (a) Calculate the component of the car's weight:
   (i) perpendicular to the slope;
   (ii) parallel to the slope.

  (b) Find the unbalanced force acting on the car.

  (c) Draw a diagram showing all the forces acting on the car parallel with the slope.

  (d) What will be the value of the force of friction acting against the car?

1.56 A tent guy-rope is pulling on a peg in the ground. The tension in the rope is 15 N and the rope is at an angle of 25° above the horizontal.

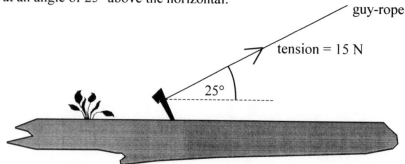

What is the value of force produced by the guy-rope on the peg in:

(i) the vertical direction;

(ii) the horizontal direction?

1.57 A trolley is being pulled up a slope by a string which is hung over a pulley and to which is attached a 1·5 kg mass. The trolley is pulled up the slope at a steady speed of 1 m s^{-1}.

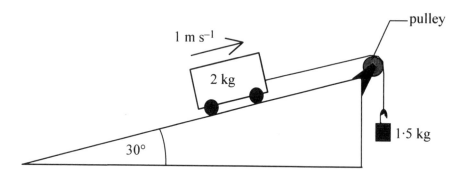

(a) What will be the component of the trolley's weight acting parallel with the slope?

(b) What will be the weight of the 1·5 kg mass?

(c) What will be the tension in the string attached to the mass?

(d) Find the force of friction acting against the trolley.

Momentum and Impulse

Momentum

1.58 A car with a mass of 1200 kg is travelling at 8 m s^{-1}. Calculate the momentum of the car.

1.59 A girl is cycling at 3 m s^{-1} and has a momentum of 180 kg m s^{-1}. What is the mass of the girl and her bicycle?

1.60 How fast is a ball travelling if it has a momentum of 1·6 kg m s^{-1} and a mass of 80 g?

1.61 Two motorists are rather angry when they collide head on. Car A is travelling at 3 m s^{-1} to the right and has a mass of 800 kg. Car B was stationary and has a mass of 1200 kg. When they collide the cars lock together. What was the velocity of the cars after the collision?

1.62 A trolley with a mass of 1·0 kg travelling at 5 m s^{-1} collides with a second stationary trolley which has a mass of 1·5 kg. After the collision the trolleys remain locked together. Calculate the velocity of the trolleys after the collision.

1.63 A child's game consists of using an elastic-powered gun to fire sticky shapes at a 'dartboard'. The mass of each of the shapes is 60 g. The board they are fired at is hanging freely and has a mass of 1·2 kg.

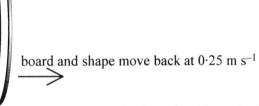

board and shape move back at 0·25 m s^{-1}

When the shape hits the board this starts to move backwards with a velocity of 0·25 m s^{-1}. Calculate the velocity with which the shape was fired.

1.64 A dog with a mass of 15 kg jumps forwards at 0·50 m s^{-1} to catch a frisbee coming in the opposite direction at a velocity of 5 m s^{-1}. The dog catches the frisbee in its mouth and in doing so its velocity drops to 0·45 m s^{-1}.

frisbee travelling at 5 m s^{-1} ⟶   ⟵ dog travelling at 0·50 m s^{-1}

What was the mass of the frisbee?

1.65 A trolley approaches another trolley head on as shown in the diagram below. Trolley A, with a mass of 3 kg and travelling at 4 m s⁻¹, has a spring attached to its front so that when it collides with trolley B they spring apart. The second trolley is stationary and has a mass of 2 kg.

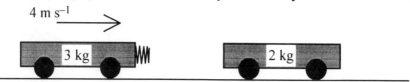

Use the principle of conservation of momentum to calculate the velocity of trolley B after the collision if trolley A continues to the right at 0·5 m s⁻¹.

1.66 In a game of snooker a ball with a mass of 0·1 kg and travelling at 0·2 m s⁻¹ collides with an identical ball which is stationary. If the first ball rebounds with a velocity of 0·1 m s⁻¹, what will be the velocity of the second ball?

1.67 A linear air track is set up to provide a frictionless surface. On the track are two vehicles which approach each other from opposite ends of the track. Vehicle 1 has a mass of 0·5 kg and travels to the right at 0·3 m s⁻¹. Vehicle 2 has a mass of 0·75 kg and travels from right to left at 0·5 m s⁻¹. Each vehicle has a spring attached to its front so that they bounce apart after colliding.

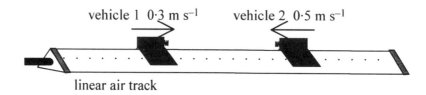

After the collision, vehicle 2 travels to the left with a velocity of 0·1 m s⁻¹. What will be the velocity of vehicle 1?

1.68 A linear air track like that used in question **1.67** is used again with two identical vehicles, each with a mass of 0·5 kg. Both vehicles have springs on their front and they are held in close contact with the springs compressed. When they are released this causes them to spring apart.

If vehicle 1 springs backwards at 0·6 m s⁻¹, what will be the velocity of vehicle 2?

1.69 A pupil recalls an experiment performed in his Standard Grade Physics class where a rocket was propelled upwards by pushing water out from its nozzle.

The empty rocket has a mass of 0·1 kg and the water contained within it has a mass of 0·8 kg. When the rocket is fired the water has an average velocity of 12 m s⁻¹ backwards. What will be the change in the forward velocity of the rocket as a result?

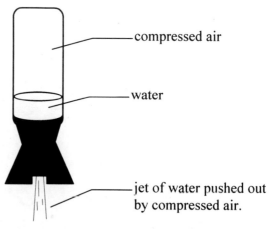

1.70 A bomb explodes into two equal halves. One half moves to the right at 30 m s^{-1}. The other half moves off to the left.

Explain, using the principal of the conservation of momentum, how it is possible to give a figure for the velocity of the other half even if the mass of each half is not known.

1.71 A popular executive toy is a device known as a Newton's cradle. It consists of large metal ball bearings suspended in a row. Each ball bearing is free to move backwards and forwards being suspended by strong thread. The mass of each ball bearing is 0·05 kg.

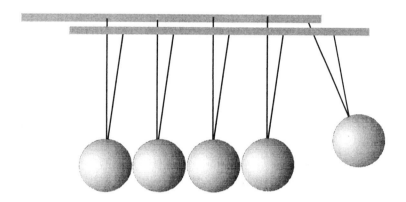

A ball bearing at the right of the cradle is pulled back and released so that it strikes the remaining stationary ball bearings with a velocity of 0·1 m s^{-1}. It then stops and the ball bearing at the left of the cradle now moves off at 0·1 m s^{-1}.

(a) Newton's cradle is an example of the principle of the conservation of momentum. State this principle.

(b) (i) Show, by suitable calculations, whether or not kinetic energy has been conserved in this collision.

(ii) State whether the collision taking place is elastic or inelastic.

1.72 Two football players jump into the air to head a ball but instead collide in mid-air. Player B, jumping to the left, has a forward velocity of 3 m s^{-1} and a mass of 65 kg. Player A, jumping to the right, has a forward velocity of 2 m s^{-1} and a mass of 75 kg.

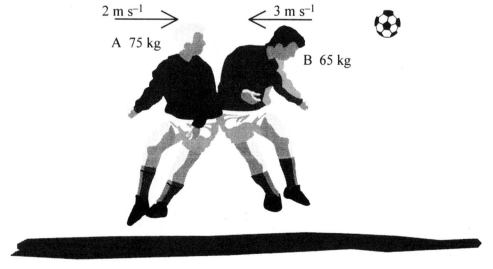

© P&N Publications

1.72 (continued)

After the collision player B continues to the left with a velocity of 0·5 m s⁻¹.

(a) Determine the velocity of player A after the collision.

(b) (i) Prove, by carrying out suitable calculations, that the collision was inelastic.

  (ii) What happens to kinetic energy lost in the above collision?

Impulse

1.73 Complete the following table by calculating the missing values.

	Impulse	Force	Time	Change in momentum
(a)		5 N	0·8 s	
(b)	30 N s	6 N		
(c)			40 ms	20×10^{-3} kg m s⁻¹
(d)	2 N s		0·01 s	

1.74 Find the impulse when a force of 30 N is applied for 0·2 s.

1.75 A ball is struck with a force of 40 N. For what length of time is contact made with the ball if it gains an impulse of 32 N s?

1.76 A volleyball player strikes a volleyball which has a mass of 0·29 kg. The force/time graph below shows how the force she applied varied with time.

(a) Calculate the total impulse applied to the volleyball.

(b) (i) What was the change in momentum of the volleyball?

  (ii) What was the change in velocity of the volleyball as a result of it being hit by the player?

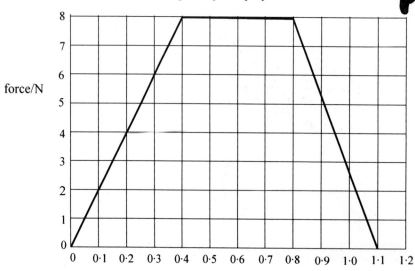

1.77 (*a*) The area beneath a child's swing in a playground is surfaced with concrete. In order to make it safer the concrete is removed and replaced with 5 cm thick rubber pads. Use a principle of physics to explain why the rubber pads provide a safer surface than the concrete surface should a child fall off the swing.

(*b*) The manufacturer of the rubber pads carries out thorough tests to ensure that the pads are hard enough to withstand the wear they will receive but will also have the correct properties for their safety function. A metal weight is dropped onto a sample of the material and force sensors measure the force acting on the weight as it strikes the pad. The graph produced for one of the materials is shown below.

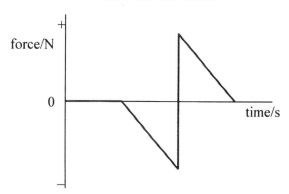

Redraw the graph above **and on the same graph**, sketch the trace which would be observed if a harder material had been under test.

1.78 A bowling ball strikes a skittle during a bowling game. The ball has a mass of 5 kg and the skittle has a mass of 1 kg. The skittle and ball are in contact for a time of 0·15 s and after being struck the skittle moves off with a velocity of 1·5 m s^{-1} and the ball continues forwards at 2·3 m s^{-1}.

(*a*) (i) Calculate the impulse acting on the skittle.

(ii) What was the average force acting on the skittle?

(*b*) As a result of the collision, what was the deceleration of the bowling ball?

(*c*) Find the speed of the ball before the collision.

Density and Pressure

Density of gases, liquids and solids

1.79 Find the missing entries in the following table for the densities of different substances. Note that density is measured in kg m^{-3} which means that mass should be in kg and volume in m^3. (1 cm^3 = 1 × 10^{-6} m^3)

	Substance	Mass	Volume	Density
(a)	Air	1·50 × 10^{-3} kg	1·16 × 10^{-3} m^3	
(b)	Hydrogen		0·005 m^3	0·09 kg m^{-3}
(c)	Iron	500 kg		7870 kg m^{-3}
(d)	Cork		1500 cm^3	240 kg m^{-3}
(e)	Lead	1000 kg		11 350 kg m^{-3}

1.80 A balloon at sea-level is filled with air which has a density of 1·2 kg m^{-3}. The balloon has a volume of 3 m^3. Calculate the mass of the air contained in the balloon.

1.81 Two liquids with different densities are mixed together. Liquid A has a volume of 2 litres and a mass of 2 kg. Liquid B has a volume of 3 litres and a mass of 2·6 kg. Calculate the density of the mixture of these two liquids.

1.82 A beaker of water is found to hold 100 cm^3 of liquid.

(a) If the density of the water is 1000 kg m^{-3}, find its mass.

(b) When water is frozen it expands slightly. How will the density of ice compare with that of water?

(c) A 0·5 kg block of ice is found to measure 6 cm by 8 cm by 11 cm. What is the density of this ice?

1.83 Judith is given an old gold necklace by her grandmother. She knows that gold has a density of 19 300 kg m^{-3}. Explain how she could use a measuring cylinder and sensitive balance to determine whether or not the necklace is pure gold.

1.84 An old oil can is sealed with a stopper and a pipe leading from the can is connected to an air pump. Air is pumped into the can and its mass measured.

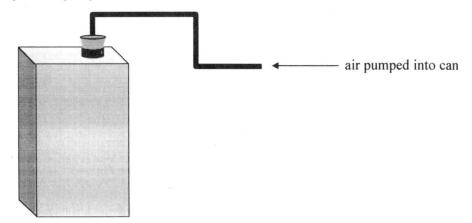

The pipe from the can is now placed under an upturned measuring cylinder full of water and the excess gas from the can allowed to expand into this. The mass of the can is now measured again.

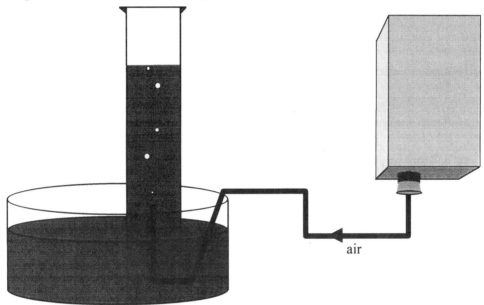

The results from this experiment are shown below.

mass of can before release of excess air	385·260 kg
mass of can after release of excess air	385·258 kg
volume of air released	$1·6 \times 10^{-3}$ m³

(a) (i) Explain how the apparatus described above can be used to find the density of the air contained in the can.

(ii) Use the results to find the density of the air.

(b) The experiment is repeated on a very warm day. How would this affect the value obtained for the density of air?

(c) The upturned measuring cylinder full of water is used in a second experiment. A 1 cm³ block of solid carbon dioxide (dry ice) is placed in the water below the measuring cylinder. As the carbon dioxide changes to gas this is collected in the measuring cylinder.

(i) Approximately what volume of gas is likely to be collected in the measuring cylinder?

(ii) What does the answer to (c) (i) tell us about the relative separation of solid and gas molecules?

Pressure, force and area

1.85 Find the missing entries in the following table:

	Pressure	Force	Area
(a)		100 N	0·05 m²
(b)		1·5 × 10³ N	0·1 m²
(c)	1 × 10⁵ Pa		1 cm²
(d)	1 × 10⁵ Pa		30 mm²
(e)	20 kPa	1250 N	

1.86 A 1 kg mass is resting on the top of a laboratory bench. If the base of the mass covers 0·01 m², find the pressure under the mass due to its weight.

1.87 A drawing pin has a point which is 0·1 mm².

  (a) Convert the area of the point into m².

  (b) What will be the pressure below the point when the pin is pressed with a force of 15 N?

1.88 (a) The pressure caused by the atmosphere at sea level is 100 kPa. What is this pressure when measured in N m⁻²?

  (b) What will be the force exerted by the atmosphere on a sheet of paper measuring 10 cm by 15 cm at sea level?

1.89 A ballerina pirouettes on one toe.

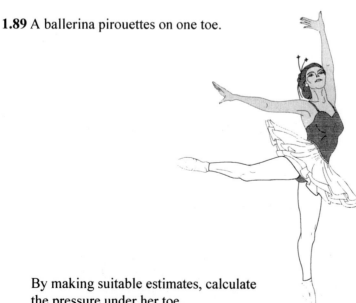

By making suitable estimates, calculate the pressure under her toe.

Buoyancy

1.90 Copy and complete the graphs below to show the relationship between:

(a) pressure and depth in a liquid of constant density;

(b) pressure and density at a constant depth.

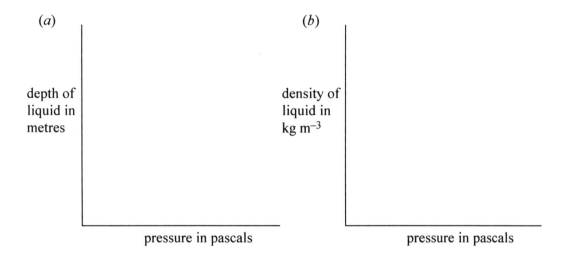

1.91 A tropical fish in an aquarium is able to control its buoyancy so that it can rest motionless in mid-water.

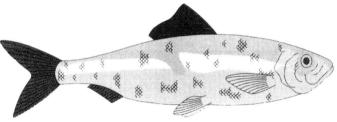

(a) Draw a diagram to show the vertical forces acting on the fish.

(b) Explain how the **buoyancy force** on the fish is produced.

1.92 A winemaker uses a device called an hydrometer to measure the density of wine. It consists of a weighted glass bulb which floats in the wine. A scale marked on the stem of the hydrometer indicates the density of the wine.

The density of alcohol is 789 kg m^{-3} and the density of water is 1000 kg m^{-3}.

What would happen to the position of the hydrometer if the proportion of alcohol in the wine increased? Explain your answer.

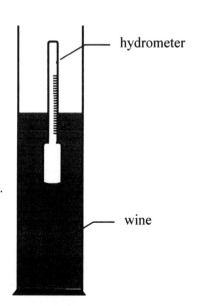

1.93 A hot air balloon rises because its weight plus the weight of the hot air inside is less than the weight of cool air displaced.

The density of the hot air in the balloon is 0·75 kg m^{-3} and the surrounding cool air has a density of 1·2 kg m^{-3}.

(a) Find the total mass which can be lifted, including the balloon itself, if the balloon has a volume of 700 m^3.

(b) The balloon rises upwards into the upper atmosphere where air is less dense. What effect will this have on the ability of the balloon to float upwards? Explain your answer.

(c) Suggest a way in which the balloon could be made to achieve a higher altitude.

1.94 A hot air balloon is tethered to the ground by a rope as shown in the diagram below. The balloon has a mass of 180 kg and produces an uplift of 2000 N.

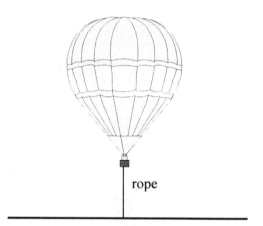

(a) Calculate the tension in the rope attached to the balloon.

(b) The rope is now released. What will be the upward acceleration of the balloon?

The Gas Laws

Pressure and volume

1.95 Find the missing entries in the following table for containers of gas where the gas has a fixed mass and is at a constant temperature.

	Pressure p_1	Volume V_1	Pressure p_2	Volume V_2
(a)	100 kPa	0·5 m^3	400 kPa	
(b)	5 × 10^5 Pa	1 m^3		0·2 m^3
(c)	15 N m^{-2}		5 N m^{-2}	50 cm^3
(d)		2 litres	1 × 10^5 Pa	10 litres
(e)	50 kPa	0·01 m^3		0·5 m^3

1.96 A Cylinder of gas contains 0·001 m^3 of gas at a pressure of 3·5 × 10^6 Pa. What volume would the gas occupy were it to be at atmospheric pressure of 1·0 × 10^5 Pa?

1.97 An experiment is carried out to show the relationship between the pressure and volume of a fixed mass of gas. The apparatus used is shown below.

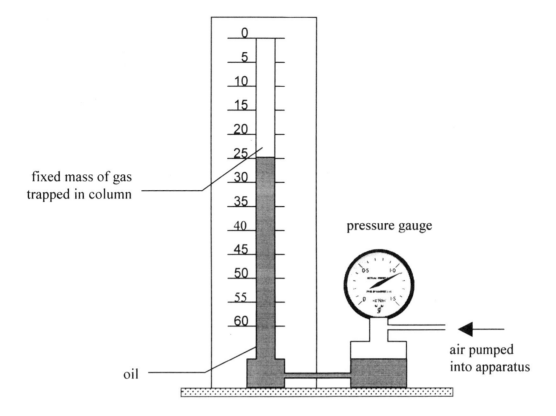

The following results are obtained from the experiment:

Pressure of air in kPa.	100	117	140	175	233	350	700
Volume of air in m³.	0·0035	0·0030	0·0025	0·0020	0·0015	0·0010	0·0005

(a) **Plot a graph** of the results in order to show a relationship between the pressure and volume of a fixed mass of gas.

(b) Explain how the molecules of air in the gas column cause an increase in pressure as the volume decreases.

(c) When the air in the column is compressed its temperature rises slightly. What precautions could be taken to ensure this does not affect the experiment?

1.98 A pupil places her finger over the end of a bicycle pump and then pushes the handle in. Explain, by using the kinetic model of gases, why this produces a rise in pressure within the pump.

1.99 A bicycle pump has a volume of 80 cm³ when it is full of air at a pressure of 1×10^5 Pa. What will be the new pressure in the pump when the plunger is pushed in and its volume becomes 2 cm³?

© P&N Publications

Pressure and temperature

1.100 Two pupils are given the apparatus shown below so that they can find the relationship between the pressure and temperature of a gas.

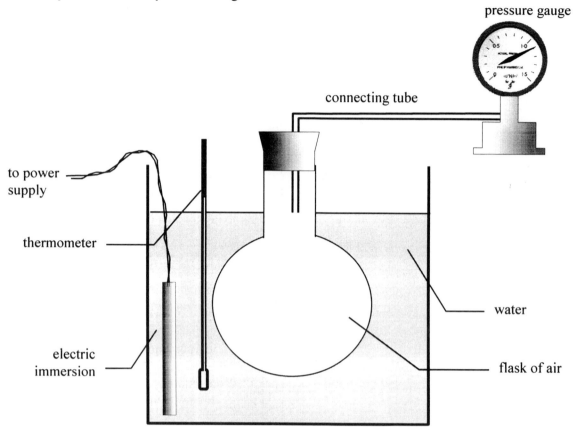

(a) Describe how the pupils would use the apparatus to find the information they need from the experiment.

(b) There are **two** factors which have to be kept constant during then experiment. State what these are.

(c) Describe **two** ways in which the experiment could be improved to give better results.

(d) The pupils' results from an improved experiment are given in the table below.

Pressure of gas in Pa.	100 000	104 000	107 000	111 000	114 000	118 000	121 000
Temperature of gas in °C	10°C	20°C	30°C	40°C	50°C	60°C	70°C

Their teacher asks them to show the relationship between temperature and pressure **without** drawing a graph i.e. it must be done by calculation. Can you show the relationship through calculation?

1.101 What is meant by the term 'absolute zero' and what is this temperature on the Celsius scale?

1.102 Find the missing entries in the following table for containers of gas where the gas has a fixed mass and is at a constant volume.

	Pressure p_1	Temperature T_1	Pressure p_2	Temperature T_2
(a)	2×10^5 Pa	400 K		600 K
(b)	100 kPa	300 K	200 kPa	
(c)	$1 \cdot 2 \times 10^5$ Pa		$1 \cdot 8 \times 10^5$ Pa	127 °C
(d)		27 °C	100 kPa	846 °C
(e)	3×10^5 Pa	600 K		0 K

1.103 A quantity of gas with a fixed volume is at a pressure of $5 \cdot 0 \times 10^5$ Pa at a temperature of 27 °C. What will be the new pressure of this gas if its temperature is increased to 227 °C with no change in its volume?

1.104 An empty aerosol canister is incinerated with some rubbish. This can withstand a pressure of 5×10^5 Pa before it bursts.

(a) Why is it wrong to describe the aerosol as being 'empty'?

(b) If the aerosol contains gas at a pressure of 1×10^5 Pa at 17 °C, what will be the temperature of the aerosol when it bursts?

1.105 A young sub-aqua diver wants to find out the effect water temperature has on the pressure inside his air cylinder. He reads the pressure inside his air cylinder in a warm car. He then places his cylinder below the water surface of the cold North Sea. Some time later he records the sea temperature and the pressure in his cylinder.

In the car
Pressure = 500 kPa
Temperature = 27 °C

In the water
Pressure = ?
Temperature = 7 °C

(a) What would be the new reading on the pressure gauge, assuming that no air had leaked from the cylinder?

(b) Explain why was it necessary for the diver to wait before reading the pressure in the water.

(c) What factors were being kept constant during the diver's experiment which could have affected his results?

© P&N Publications

1.106 A gas cylinder used for making fizzy drinks contains 400 cm³ of carbon dioxide at a pressure of 1000 kPa.

    (*a*) What will be the volume of gas contained in the cylinder if it was allowed to expand at atmospheric pressure of 100 kPa?

    (*b*) Explain why gas trapped in a cylinder produces pressure on the cylinder walls.

    (*c*) A cylinder is left on a windowsill in the sun which causes its temperature to rise.

        (i) What effect has this on the pressure within the cylinder?

        (ii) Explain this change in terms of the movement of gas molecules.

Volume and Temperature

1.107 A quantity of gas is held in a sealed container at 20 °C. What will be the temperature of this gas on the Kelvin scale?

1.108 Find the missing entries in the following table for containers of gas where the gas has a fixed mass and is at a constant pressure.

	Volume V_1	Temperature T_1	Volume V_2	Temperature T_2
(*a*)	0·5 m³	200 K		800 K
(*b*)	6 litres		1·5 litres	300 K
(*c*)	4 litres	27 °C		127 °C
(*d*)		27 °C	5 m³	327 °C
(*e*)	4 litres	0 °C	30 litres	

1.109 A balloon is filled with air at a temperature of 27 °C to a volume of 5 litres. What will be the new volume of the balloon if it is placed in the sun and the temperature of the gas it contained rose to 42 °C?

1.110 A sealed syringe contains 20 cm³ of air at a temperature of 20 °C. The syringe is then placed into a water bath at 90 °C. What will be the new volume occupied by the gas assuming there is no change in pressure?

1.111 (*a*) Use the kinetic model of gases to explain why the volume of a fixed mass of gas decreases as the temperature of the gas decreases.

    (*b*) If a gas were to be cooled down to absolute zero it would, in theory, have no volume.

        (i) What is the temperature of absolute zero in
           A   the Celsius temperature scale;
           B   the Kelvin temperature scale?

        (ii) Explain why it would never be possible to cool down a gas to zero volume.

1.112 An experiment is carried out to investigate the relationship between the volume and temperature of a gas. The apparatus used is shown below. A column of gas is trapped by a bead of mercury and this is placed in a water bath. As the temperature of the surrounding water increases the water temperature is taken and the length of the trapped gas is recorded. The length of this trapped gas is proportional to its volume.

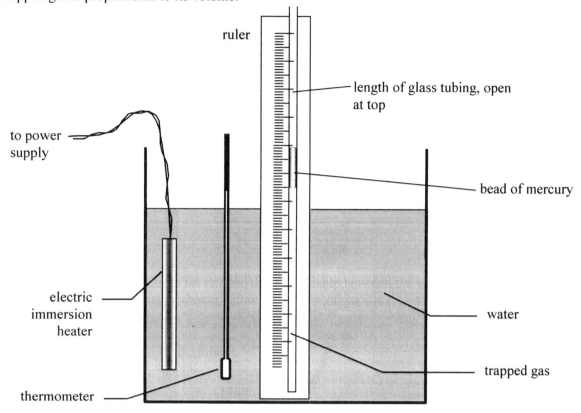

The results obtained from the experiment are given in the table below.

Length of tube/cm	21·5	22·9	24·4	25·9	27·3
Temperature of water °C	20	40	60	80	100

(a) Explain why the tube containing the gas must be kept open.

(b) Use the results given above to show the relationship between the volume and temperature of the gas.

(c) Suggest **two** improvements which could be made to the experimental apparatus to improve the accuracy of the results obtained.

(d) Ice and salt are added to the water until the temperature is reduced. What will be the temperature of the gas when the gas column has a length of 19·5 cm?

(e) An observer states that the gas trapped in the tube is at atmospheric pressure. State why this is not totally correct.

The General Gas Equation

1.113 State the general gas equation.

1.114 Find the missing entries in the following table for containers of gas where the gas always has a fixed mass.

	Pressure p_1	Volume V_1	Temperature T_1	Pressure p_2	Volume V_2	Temperature T_2
(a)	1.0×10^5 Pa	0.5 m³	200 K	5.0×10^5 Pa		600 K
(b)	1.0×10^5 Pa	2 litres	400 K		0.05 litres	500 K
(c)	2.5×10^5 Pa	5 litres	200 K	30×10^5 Pa	0.05 litres	
(d)	1.0×10^5 Pa	4 litres	27 °C	2.0×10^5 Pa		127 °C
(e)		0.2 m³	27 °C	5.0×10^5 Pa	5 m³	327 °C
(f)	100 kPa	4 litres		400 kPa	30 litres	187 °C

1.115 A fixed mass of gas has a volume of 3 litres and a pressure of 200 kPa when at a temperature of 27 °C. What will be the volume of the gas when it is at a pressure of 100 kPa and its temperature is increased to 327 °C?

1.116 A bubble of gas rises from the sea floor where it is at a pressure of 30×10^6 Pa and is at a temperature of 1 °C. The bubble has a volume of 1×10^{-9} m³. What volume will the bubble occupy at the surface of the sea where the pressure is 1.0×10^5 Pa and the temperature is 12 °C?

1.117 A balloon containing helium is released from the ground where the temperature is 27 °C and the air pressure is 1.0×10^5 Pa. The gas contained in the balloon has a volume of 2 m³. What will be the temperature of the helium when it has risen to a high altitude where the pressure of the gas has decreased to 1.83×10^4 Pa and the volume of the balloon is now 8.4 m³?

1.118 A fixed mass of gas is at a pressure of 2.0×10^5 Pa. What will be the new pressure of the gas if the temperature of the gas in Kelvin is doubled and the volume the gas occupies is halved?

UNIT 2 Electricity and Electronics

Electric Fields and Resistors in Circuits

Electric fields

2.1 An electric field exists between two metal plates as shown below.

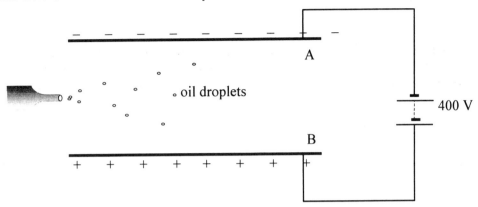

Small oil droplets are sprayed into the space between the plates.

(a) A droplet is observed to slowly travel upwards towards plate A. State **two** forces which must be acting on the oil droplet.

(b) What electrical charge must the oil drop have?

2.2 Complete the following table by filling in the missing values.

	Work	Charge	Voltage
(a)		5 mC	100 V
(b)		100 µC	2000 V
(c)	0·1 mJ	2 C	
(d)	5 J		5 kV

2.3 A car engine uses a spark plug to ignite the air–petrol mixture in the engine. A spark crosses the end of the spark plug in a time of $1·25 \times 10^{-4}$ s.

(a) (i) The average current which flows when the spark crosses the gap is 80 mA. What is the total charge transferred as a result of one spark?

(ii) How many electrons cross the gap for each spark?

(b) What work is done in transferring a spark across the gap if the voltage across the spark plug is 500 V? [You may require to use data from the data sheet in Appendix (ii).]

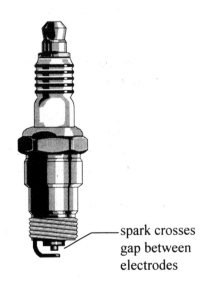

© P&N Publications

2.4 An electron is accelerated towards the screen of a television tube by a potential difference of 22 kV.

(a) What will be the work done on the electron?

(b) Assuming the electron starts from rest, what will be the final speed reached by the electron?

2.5 An oscilloscope produces a stream of electrons from a hot filament. The electrons are then accelerated by a high voltage connected between the cathode and anode. The electron beam is directed towards the oscilloscope screen but can be deflected up or down by a voltage applied to the plates Y_1 and Y_2.

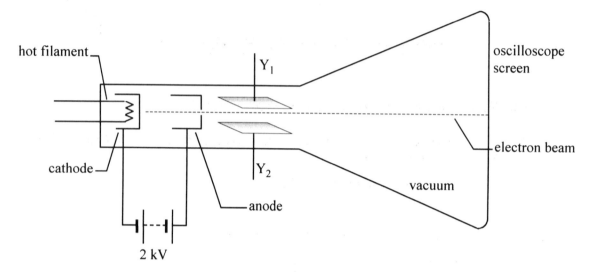

(a) What work is done in accelerating an electron across the 2 kV?

(b) What is the total kinetic energy of the electron when it leaves the anode?

(c) What will be the velocity of the electron on leaving the anode?

(d) To which plate, Y_1 or Y_2, should the positive connection be applied to make the beam deflect upwards? Explain your answer.

(e) The oscilloscope tube has to be a vacuum. Suggest a reason for this.

E.m.f. and internal resistance

2.6 State which of the following provide a source of an electromotive force (e.m.f.):

(i) car battery;
(ii) solar cell;
(iii) light emitting diode;
(iv) bicycle dynamo;
(v) transistor;
(vi) thermocouple.

2.7 A text book quotes the formula:

$$E = I(R + r)$$

(a) State the meaning of each of the symbols used in the formula.

(b) Explain how this formula can be used to justify, by the conservation of energy, that the e.m.f. of a circuit is equal to the sum of the potential differences around the circuit.

2.8 Find the missing entries in the following table.

	E.m.f.	Current	External resistance	Internal resistance
(a)		0·5 A	20 Ω	2 Ω
(b)	12 V	200 mA	55 Ω	
(c)	1·5 V	50 mA		0·7 Ω
(d)	9 V		15 Ω	3 Ω

2.9 A cell has an e.m.f. of 1·5 V and an internal resistance of 0·5 Ω. What current is being drawn if the voltage across the cell drops to 1·4 V?

2.10 A 10 Ω resistor is connected in series with a cell of e.m.f. 6 V and with an internal resistance of 2 Ω.

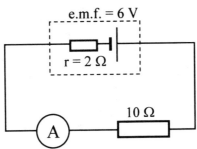

(a) Find the current flowing through the ammeter.

(b) What will be the voltage across the terminals of the cell?

(c) What is the value of the lost volts in the circuit?

2.11 A 5 Ω resistor is connected to a cell which has an e.m.f. of 1·5 V and an internal resistance of 0·5 Ω.

(a) What will be the current flowing around the circuit?

(b) What electrical power will be dissipated:
   (i) in the external resistance;
   (ii) in the internal resistance of the cell?

2.12 A cell with an e.m.f. of 1·5 V is bought and used to power a small torch.

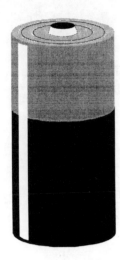

(a) State how the e.m.f. of the cell could be measured.

(b) (i) Draw a circuit which could be used to find the internal resistance of the cell using apparatus commonly available in a school physics laboratory.

(ii) State how the internal resistance of the cell would be calculated.

(c) The voltage across the cell is found to be 1·36 V when a current of 150 mA is being drawn. Find the internal resistance of the cell.

2.13 A circuit is set up to investigate the properties of a cell. A variable resistor connected to the cell allows different values of current in the circuit.

The current and corresponding voltage across the cell is measured and a graph plotted from the values obtained.

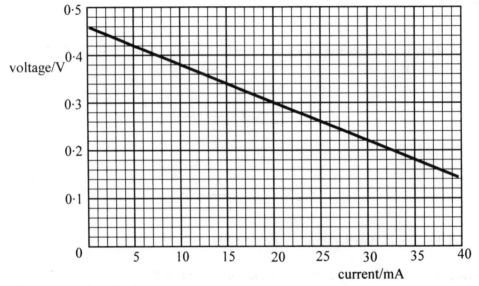

(a) Use the graph to find:

(i) the e.m.f. of the cell;

(ii) the internal resistance of the cell.

(b) (i) State how it would be possible to 'short–circuit' a cell.

(ii) What current would leave the cell were it to be short–circuited?

© P&N Publications

2.14 A bulb rated at 9 V, 0·3 A is connected to a 9 V cell. When this is done the voltage across the cell is found to be only 8·4 V.

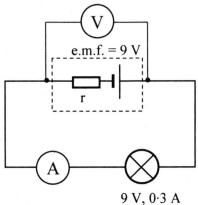

(a) Explain why the voltage across the cell drops to 8·4 V.

(b) Calculate the internal resistance of the cell.

2.15 A cell is placed in a circuit as shown below.

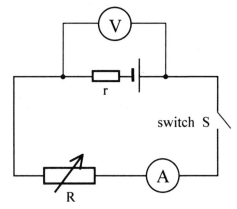

The following data was obtained during an experiment using the circuit.

    Switch S open:
        ammeter reading = 0 mA
        voltmeter reading = 1·45 V

    Switch S closed
        ammeter reading = 180 mA
        voltmeter reading = 1·39 V

(a) What is the e.m.f. of the cell?

(b) Find the internal resistance of the cell.

(c) If the value of the variable resistor is decreased what effect would this have on:

    (i) the ammeter reading;

    (ii) the 'lost volts' in the circuit;

    (iii) the voltmeter reading?

2.16 A car battery has an e.m.f. of 12 V. The manufacturer also quotes the battery as being rated at 60 A h which means that the battery can supply 60 A for 1 hour or, for example, 20 A for 3 hours.

(a) (i) What is the total charge available from the battery assuming it is fully charged to the manufacturer's specification?

(ii) What is the electrical energy available from the battery if its terminal potential difference was to remain constant at 12 V?

(b) The battery is made up of 6 identical cells, each with an e.m.f. of 2 V. When connected together in series they provide the total battery e.m.f. of 12 V.

The battery is attached to a car which draws a current of 80 A when it is being started. If the battery voltage drops to 9 V at this time calculate:

(i) the total internal resistance of the battery;

(ii) the internal resistance of each cell;

(iii) the power dissipated as heat within the battery.

(c) The internal resistance of a cell increases as the temperature of the cells decreases. A graph of this is shown below.

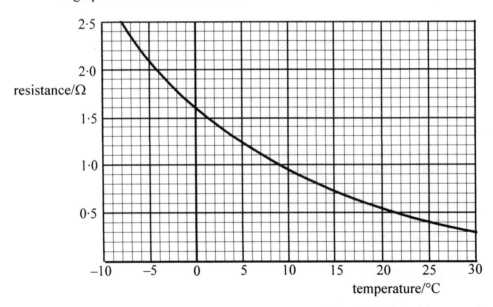

(i) Find the internal resistance of a cell at:

A   −5 °C;

B   25 °C.

(ii) A motorist finds that she has difficulty starting her car during cold winter mornings. Explain this observation by making reference to the internal resistance of the battery.

Resistors in circuits

2.17 A circuit is set up with three resistors in series.

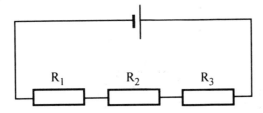

Show, by consideration of the conservation of energy, that for the above circuit

$$R_{TOTAL} = R_1 + R_2 + R_3.$$

2.18 A circuit is set up with three resistors in parallel.

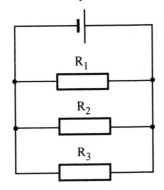

Show, by consideration of the conservation of charge, that for the above circuit

$$\frac{1}{R_{TOTAL}} = \frac{1}{R_1} + \frac{1}{R_2} + \frac{1}{R_3}.$$

2.19 Find the total resistance of the following circuits.

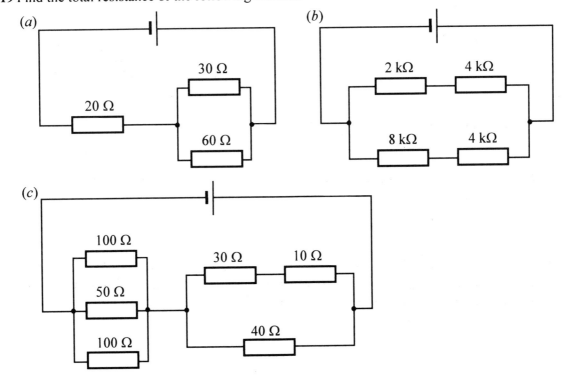

2.20 A circuit is set up using a 1·5 V cell with negligible internal resistance.

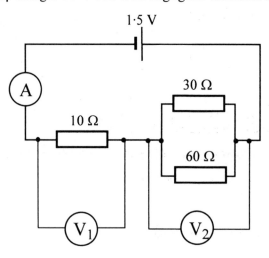

(a) What current would the ammeter read in the circuit above?

(b) Find the value of the voltages V_1 and V_2.

(c) What current will flow through:
   (i) the 30 Ω resistor;
   (ii) the 60 Ω resistor?

(d) Find the total power dissipated by the circuit.

2.21 A potential divider circuit is set up to provide a range of voltages. A voltmeter can be placed across any single resistor or combination of resistors. The cell has negligible internal resistance.

(a) To which two connections would the voltmeter be connected to obtain:
   (i) the maximum voltage available from this circuit;
   (ii) the minimum voltage available from this circuit?

(b) What will be the power developed in the 150 Ω resistor?

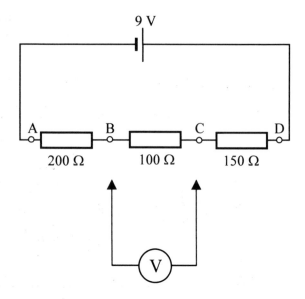

2.22 An overhead power cable is made up of 12 strands of aluminium placed side by side and twisted together. Each strand has a resistance of 4×10^{-8} Ω per metre. What would be the total resistance of a length of the cable which is 1 km long?

2.23 A potential divider circuit is used to split the voltage from a 12 V power supply.

(a) What will be the voltage between:

(i) A and B;

(ii) B and C?

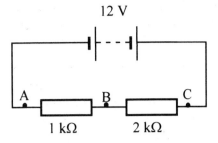

(b) An 500 Ω resistor is now placed in parallel with the first. What is new voltage between:

(i) A and B;

(ii) B and C?

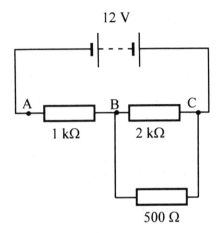

2.24 A pupil takes a complete loop of wire and connects an ohmmeter to two points, A and B, which have equal lengths of wire between them. The ohmmeter reads 15·0 Ω.

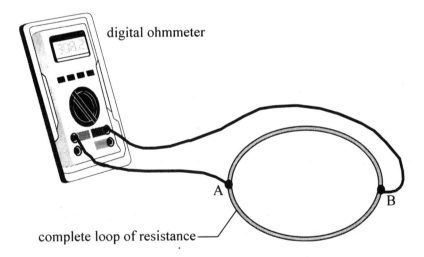

(a) The contact at A is slowly moved along the wire towards B. State whether the ohmmeter reading will increase, decrease or remain the same. Justify your answer.

(b) One side of the loop is cut when A and B are equal distances apart. What will the ohmmeter now read?

© P&N Publications

2.25 A pupil is given a sealed box by his teacher and told that it contains four resistors, two 10 Ω and two 2 Ω, connected up as shown below. There are four connections to which he can attach an ohmmeter but one lead is permanently fixed to terminal A. The table below lists the measurements he was able to make.

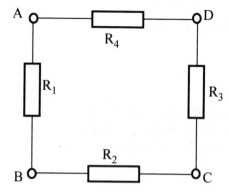

Connector positions	Ohm–meter reading
AB	5·8 Ω
AC	3·3 Ω
AD	1·8 Ω

Deduce the value of each of the resistors R_1 to R_4.

2.26 A dimmer circuit is required for a low voltage light bulb in a doll's house. To achieve this a physics pupil designs two circuits, one using a potentiometer and the other a variable resistor.

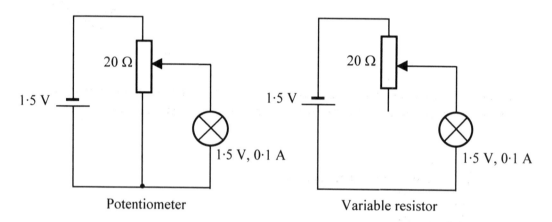

Potentiometer   Variable resistor

Identical lamps are used in the circuits and these are rated at 1·5 V, 0·1 A.

(a) What is the resistance of the lamps being used?

(b) Which circuit is capable of being adjusted so that practically **no current** flows through the bulb?

(c) The circuits are adjusted to give so that the bulbs are at their maximum brightness. What would be the power produced in:

  (i) the potentiometer circuit;

  (ii) the variable resistor circuit?

(d) The pupil wishes to extend the life of the cell being used for as long as possible. Which circuit will give the longer cell life with the bulb at maximum brightness?

2.27 A pupil is trying to light a 2·5 V, 0·1 A bulb using a 6·0 V power supply. He sets up a potential divider circuit as shown below.

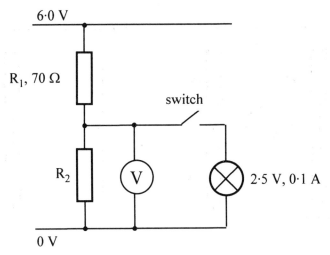

(a) What must be the voltage across R_1 if the bulb is to operate correctly?

(b) With the switch in the open position the voltmeter reads 2·5 V. What is the value of resistor R_2 at this time?

(c) The switch is now closed and it is observed that the voltmeter reading drops and the bulb is not as bright as it should be.

   (i) Explain this observation.

   (ii) Calculate the voltage now present across the bulb.

Wheatstone Bridge

2.28 A Wheatstone bridge is set up using four resistors, R_1 to R_4, as shown below.

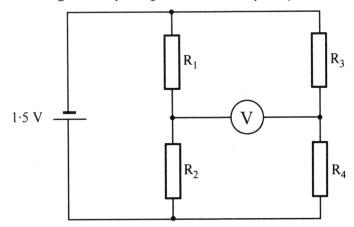

(a) State the relationship among the four resistors if the bridge is in a balanced condition.

(b) What will be the reading on the voltmeter when the bridge is balanced?

2.29 Find the resistance of the unknown resistor, R_X, in each of the balanced Wheatstone bridge circuits below.

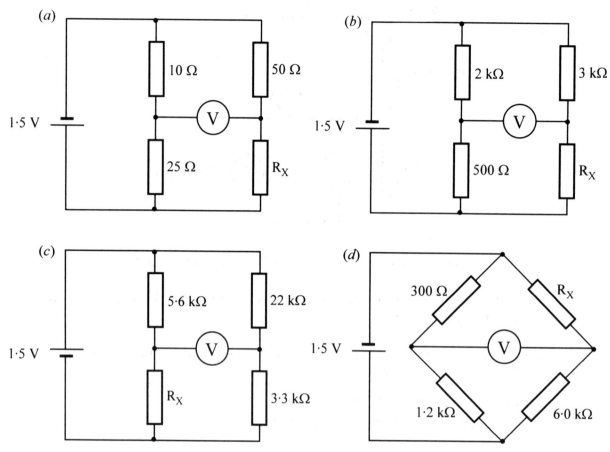

2.30 A Wheatstone bridge circuit is set up using three resistors and a light bulb. The light bulb is operating at its normal brightness and its resistance remains constant throughout the experiment. R_3 is a 0–50 Ω variable resistor.

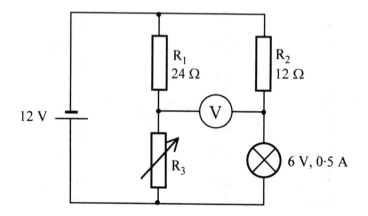

(a) What value should R_3 be set at in order to achieve a balanced bridge?

(b) The 12 V cell is now replaced with a 9 V cell.
  (i) Will the bridge still be balanced as a result of this?
  (ii) What will now be the voltage across the bulb?
  (iii) To bring the bulb back to full brightness resistor R_2 is replaced with a 6 Ω resistor. What value must R_3 be set at to regain a balanced bridge?

2.31 A pupil sets up a Wheatstone bridge circuit which includes a resistance box in one of the legs. The resistance box is capable of being set to any resistance between 1 and 10 000 Ω in 1 Ω steps.

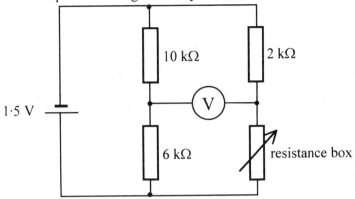

(a) What initial value must the resistance box be set at in order to produce a balanced bridge?

The bridge is balanced and then the value of the resistance box altered by either increasing or decreasing its setting in 1 Ω increments.

(b) (i) Using the axes drawn below, sketch the graph that would have been obtained from this experiment.

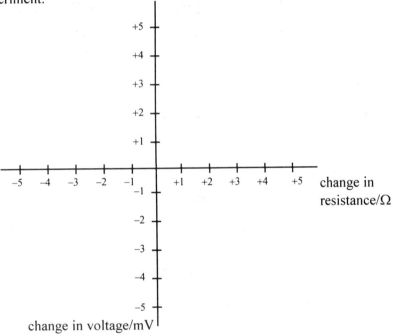

(ii) State the relationship between the change in resistance and the change in voltage.

(c) The class teacher suggests that a sensitive voltmeter would be the best choice when trying to produce a balanced bridge rather than a very accurate one. Explain why the teacher made this statement.

2.32 A thermistor is used in a Wheatstone bridge circuit to monitor small changes in the temperature of food during its processing. The table below shows the resistance of the thermistor over a range of temperatures.

Temperature	0°C	10°C	20°C	30°C	40°C
Resistance	350 kΩ	207 kΩ	127 kΩ	80 kΩ	51 kΩ

(a) Plot a graph of resistance against temperature for the thermistor.

(b) The thermistor is inserted into the circuit shown below.

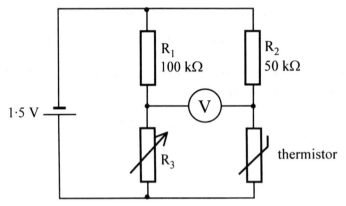

(i) At what value must the variable resistor R_3 be set in order to obtain a balanced bridge at 7°C?

(ii) Explain how the circuit could be calibrated so that the reading on the voltmeter can be used to indicate temperature.

(iii) Which of the following changes, if any, would have the effect of making the temperature measurement **more sensitive**?

    A   Increasing the voltage of the cell.

    B   Decreasing the value of R_1 and R_2 to 10 kΩ and 5 kΩ respectively.

    C   Replacing the thermistor with one which has a larger change in resistance for the same change in temperature.

Explain your answer for each of the above.

2.33 A Wheatstone bridge is constructed with a 1 m length of resistance wire replacing two of the resistors. The resistance of the wire is directly proportional to its length. This wire is divided into two sections of variable length by a sliding contact as shown opposite.

The contact is moved until the voltmeter shows a reading of zero. At this time the wire is split into two lengths, one 38 cm and the other 62 cm.

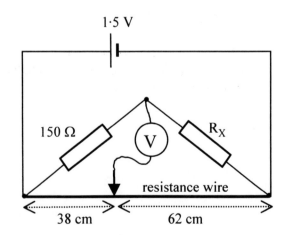

Find the resistance of the unknown resistor R_X.

2.34 A Wheatstone bridge circuit is set up to measure the intensity of light produced by several fluorescent tubes. These are thought to produce approximately the same light output but it is necessary to measure small changes in intensity between tubes. To accomplish this a light dependent resistor (LDR) is placed in one of the arms as shown below.

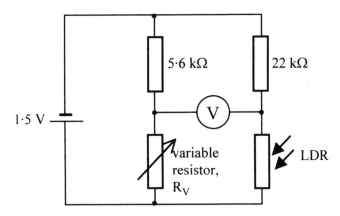

(a) The room in which the measurements were made has a level of illumination such that the LDR has a resistance of 1200 Ω. To what value should the variable resistor be set in order to achieve a balanced bridge circuit?

(b) Explain how the circuit is able to take account of any day-to-day difference in the light level from the illumination within the room.

(c) The range of frequencies produced by the visible radiation from the fluorescent tube will differ from tube to tube. The manufacturer of the LDR produces the following graph showing the response of the LDR to wavelengths of light in the range 360 – 840 nm for a constant level of illumination.

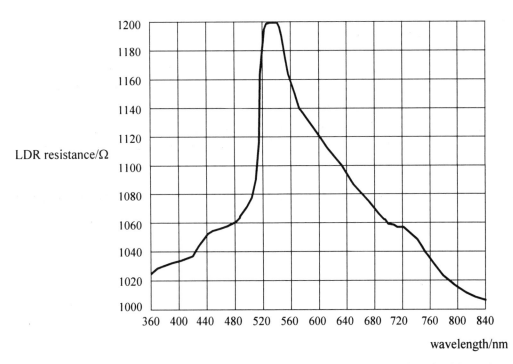

A tube which produces light with a wavelength of 480 nm is replaced with a tube producing a wavelength of 600 nm. If the bridge was initially balanced, what change in the resistance of the variable resistor is required to bring the bridge back into balance?

2.35 In a school experiment, a pupil wishes to investigate how the resistance of a thermistor varies with temperature. To obtain the necessary results he sets up a Wheatstone bridge circuit as shown below.

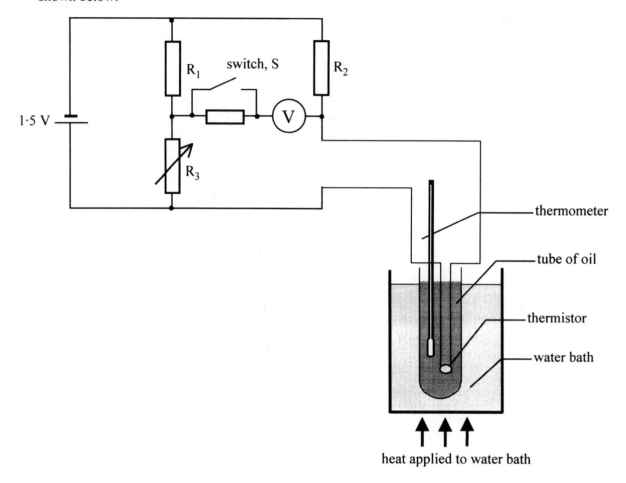

(a) Why is the thermistor placed in the oil and water bath rather than being heated directly?

(b) (i) A very sensitive voltmeter is used in the experiment and could be damaged. The pupil's teacher advises placing a high value resistor in series with the meter. Explain how this will protect the voltmeter.

  (ii) The switch, S, is present to remove the series resistor from the circuit when its presence is no longer required. Should the switch be open or closed to achieve this? Explain your answer.

(c) Explain how the pupil would use the apparatus to plot a graph of thermistor temperature against resistance.

Alternating Current and Voltage

Alternating current

2.36 An oscilloscope is used to compare the frequency of two a.c. power supplies. The oscilloscope screens are divided into 1 cm squares and these are shown below along with the timebase settings. Determine the frequency of each trace.

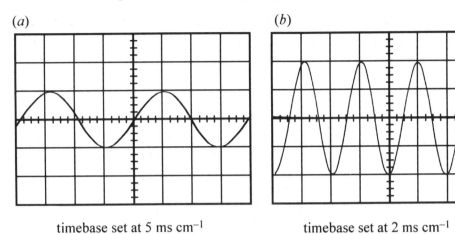

(a) timebase set at 5 ms cm⁻¹

(b) timebase set at 2 ms cm⁻¹

2.37 Mains voltage must be transmitted within a certain band of voltages. If it has an r.m.s. value of 240 V, what will be the peak voltage supplied?

2.38 An a.c. meter is used to measure the current through a resistor. The current is known to have a peak value of 280 mA. What will be the r.m.s. value indicated by the meter?

2.39 An a.c. power supply is used to light a 6 $V_{r.m.s.}$, 0·2 $A_{r.m.s.}$ light bulb. Find the peak value of voltage and current supplied to the light bulb.

2.40 The circuit shown below was set up using a signal generator as a source of varying frequency a.c. The amplitude of output was kept constant at a peak voltage 6 V at a frequency of 100 Hz.

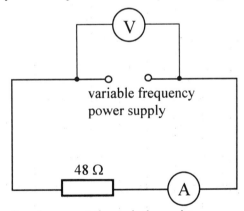

(a) Calculate the value of peak current through the resistor.

(b) What is the value of the r.m.s. current through the resistor?

(c) The frequency of the supply is increased from 100 Hz to 200 Hz. What effect will this have on the current through the resistor?

2.41 A light bulb with a resistance of 60 Ω is connected to a 12 V r.m.s. supply.

(a) What is the peak voltage of the power supply?

(b) Calculate the value of r.m.s. current flowing through the light bulb?

(c) (i) What is the r.m.s. power produced by the light bulb?

(ii) If the ac supply were to be replaced with a dc supply providing the same power output, what value of voltage would be required?

Capacitance
Charge, voltage and capacitance

2.42 A pupil sets up the circuit shown below. A capacitor is attached to a coulombmeter and variable d.c. power supply via a two-way switch. This allows the capacitor to be first connected to the power supply and then disconnected from this before being connected to the coulombmeter.

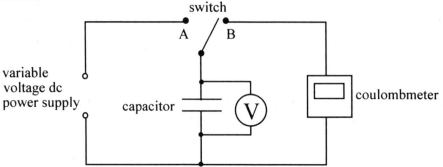

(a) The pupil uses the apparatus to produce the graph shown below. Describe how the apparatus would have been used to obtain these results.

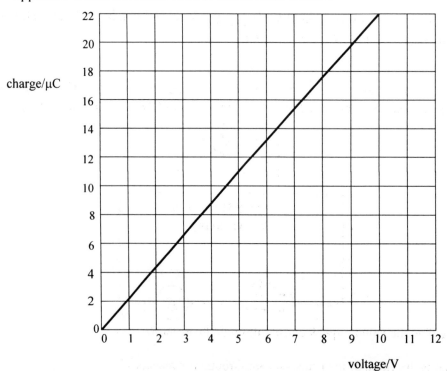

(b) State the relationship between the charge stored on a capacitor and the voltage across it.

(c) Use the graph to find the value of capacitor used in the experiment.

2.43 Complete the following table by filling in the missing values.

	Capacitance	Charge	Voltage
(a)		0·002 C	100 V
(b)		100 µC	2 kV
(c)	5 µF	120 mC	
(d)	16 µF		5 kV

2.44 A picofarad is equivalent to 1×10^{-12} F. How much charge can be stored on a 10 pF capacitor charged to a voltage of 12 V?

2.45 A capacitor stores 0·05 C of charge and has a p.d. across its plates of 20 V. What is its capacitance?

2.46 A 22 µF capacitor is charged in 55 s by an average current of 10 mA. What will be the voltage across the capacitor when it is fully charged?

2.47 A 1000 µF capacitor is charged using a 6 V power supply.

(a) What will be the voltage across the capacitor when it is fully charged?

(b) The capacitor is now discharged and this takes 20 s. What will be the average current flowing from the capacitor during the discharging process?

2.48 A circuit is set up which consists of a resistor and capacitor in series connected to a 1·5 V cell with negligible internal resistance.

(a) The switch, S, is closed and the capacitor allowed to charge. What will be the initial reading on the ammeter?

(b) Before any charge has built up on the capacitor, what will be:

(i) the initial voltage across the **capacitor**;

(ii) the initial voltage across the **resistor**?

(c) The capacitor charges to its full capacity. What will now be:

(i) the voltage across the **capacitor**;

(ii) the voltage across the **resistor**?

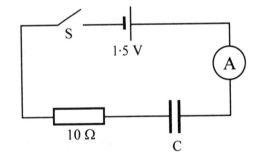

Energy stored on a capacitor

2.49 The following circuit is set up which allows a capacitor to be alternately charged and discharged. The capacitor is initially discharged.

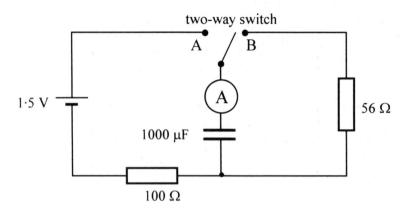

The switch is moved to position A and the capacitor allowed to charge.

(a) (i) Explain, in terms of the movement of electrons, what is happening during the charging period.

(ii) Explain why work must be done in order to charge a capacitor.

(b) The following charge/voltage graph was obtained during the charging process.

(i) What will be the charge Q, on the capacitor when it is fully charged?

(ii) Use this graph to calculate the work done in charging the capacitor.

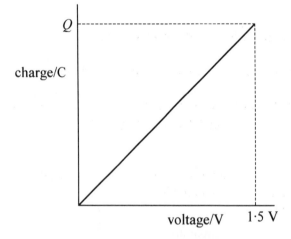

(c) The switch is now moved to position B and the capacitor discharges through the 56 Ω resistor.

(i) What will be the initial current flowing through this resistor?

(ii) What happens to the energy which was stored on the capacitor?

2.50 Combine the equation for energy stored on a capacitor $\left(E = \tfrac{1}{2}QV\right)$ with the equation for capacitance $\left(C = \dfrac{Q}{V}\right)$ to give two alternative equations for calculating the energy stored on a capacitor.

2.51 A capacitor is able to store 20 mC at a voltage of 20 V. What will be the energy stored on the capacitor?

2.52 Find the energy stored on a 1000 μF capacitor which is charged to 5 V.

2.53 In an experiment a pupil uses a 220 μF capacitor which he charges until it holds a total charge of 3×10^{-3} C. What energy will be stored by the capacitor as a result?

2.54 A capacitor is rated at allowing a maximum voltage of 16 V across it. When this voltage is applied it stores $2 \cdot 8 \times 10^{-3}$ J of energy.

   (a) What is the capacitance of the capacitor?

   (b) If an a.c. source is applied to the capacitor and the maximum voltage allowed across it is 16 V, what will be the r.m.s. value of voltage allowed?

2.55 A 100 nF capacitor is charged up until the voltage across it reaches 12 V.

   (a) What charge is stored on the capacitor?

   (b) Find the energy stored on the capacitor.

   (c) What work is done in charging the capacitor?

2.56 A capacitor of value of 500 μF and stores 64 mJ of energy.

   (a) What will be the potential difference across the capacitor?

   (b) How much charge is being stored by the capacitor?

2.57 A capacitor is charged using a power supply which provides a constant current of 0·05 mA. After 10 s the capacitor is fully charged.

   (a) Find the voltage across the capacitor if it has a capacitance of 10 μF.

   (b) How much energy is stored on the capacitor?

2.58 The electronic flash on a camera uses capacitors to store the energy used by the flash tube to produce light. The advantage of an electronic flash is that it can produce a very bright but short burst of light. The flash uses a 50 μF capacitor to store sufficient energy to deliver a power of 1 kW in 3×10^{-3} s.

   (a) What voltage will the capacitor be charged to?

   (b) What will be the charge stored on the capacitor?

Charging and discharging capacitors

2.59 A capacitor is placed in the circuit shown below. A voltmeter is connected across the capacitor so that the voltage across it can be recorded after the switch is closed.

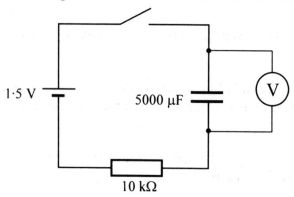

(a) Draw a voltage against time graph for the time when the switch is closed until the capacitor is fully charged. Include numerical values on the axis.

(b) Draw a graph of charge against voltage for the charging of the capacitor. Include numerical values on the axis.

2.60 A capacitor is connected in series with a resistor as shown below.

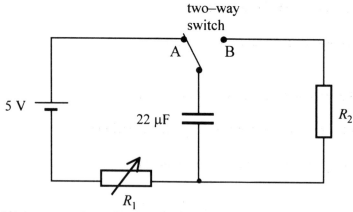

The switch is connected to A so that the capacitor charges through resistor R_1.

(a) (i) Sketch a graph of voltage against time for the charging capacitor.

(ii) Sketch a graph of current against time for the charging capacitor.

(b) The switch is now moved to position B so that the capacitor discharges through resistor R_2.

(i) Sketch a graph of voltage against time for the discharging capacitor.

(ii) Sketch a graph of current against time for the discharging capacitor.

(c) What would have been the effect on the time taken for the capacitor to become fully charged if:

(i) a capacitor with a larger value of 100 µF had been used;

(ii) the value of R_1 had been increased?

2.61 A capacitor is placed in the circuit shown below.

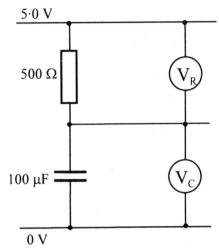

(a) (i) If the capacitor starts in an uncharged state, what will be the initial charging current?

(ii) What charge will be held by the capacitor when it is fully charged?

(iii) How much energy will be stored by the capacitor when fully charged?

(b) (i) Sketch a graph to show the change in voltage shown by the voltmeter V_C as the capacitor charges.

(ii) Sketch a graph to show the change in voltage across V_R during the same time period as (b) (i).

(c) The 500 Ω resistor is removed and replaced with a 100 Ω resistor.

(i) What effect will this change in resistance have on the time taken for the capacitor to go from being discharged to becoming fully charged?

(ii) What effect will this have on the total energy stored by the capacitor? Justify your answer.

Capacitors and a.c.
2.62 Two pupils set up a circuit to investigate the relationship between current and frequency in a capacitive circuit. Their circuit is shown opposite. The frequency of the power supply output is continuously variable.

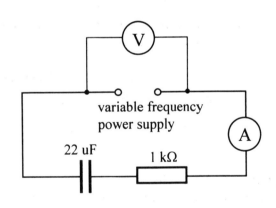

(a) Explain how the apparatus described above could be used to show the relationship between current and frequency in a capacitive circuit.

(b) One pupil expresses concern that the resistor in the circuit will have an effect on their results. Explain why this fear is unjustified.

(c) Draw a graph of current against frequency for this circuit.

2.63 A capacitor is alternately charged and discharged by placing it in the circuit shown below.

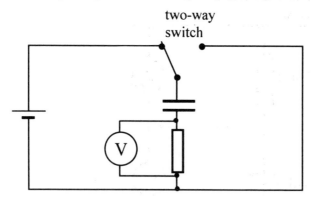

The switch is rapidly moved to and fro between the contacts of the two-way switch. A graph of the voltage across the resistor is shown below. The voltage across the resistor is proportional to the current in the circuit.

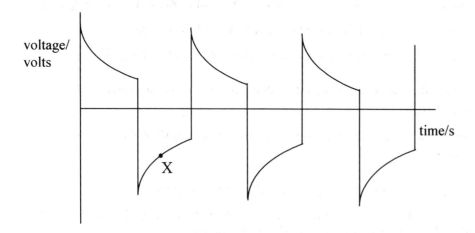

(a) Explain what is happening in the circuit at point X on the graph.

(b) (i) Explain why the graph never reaches zero volts.

(ii) Sketch the graph which would be produced if the resistor was replaced with one with less resistance.

(c) The switch now moves between the contacts at a higher frequency.

(i) What effect will this have on the current through the resistor?

(ii) Explain your answer to (c) (i).

Applications of capacitors

2.64 A potential divider circuit is set up with a resistor and a capacitor in series. The values of each are chosen so that the voltage from the power supply splits equally between the resistor and capacitor. The power supply has a frequency of 100 Hz.

The supply frequency is now increased from 100 Hz to 200 Hz. The supply voltage no longer splits evenly between the capacitor and resistor.
Explain this observation.

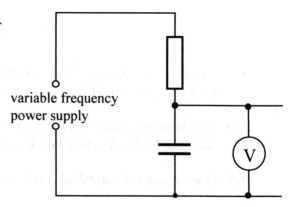

2.65 A capacitor is used as a time delay circuit in the door of a spin drier so that the door cannot be opened for several seconds after the spinning mechanism is switched off. A simplified diagram of the circuit is shown below.

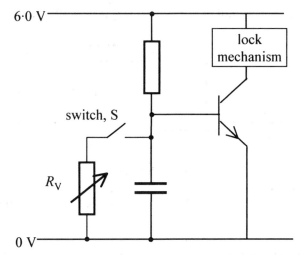

If the transistor output is high the lock mechanism prevents the door from being opened. When the spin drier is switched on the switch S, is open. When the drier is switched off the switch closes.

(a) What will be the voltage across the capacitor when the spinner is on?

(b) Explain how the capacitor operates to prevent the door being opened when the spin drier is switched off.

(c) How could the circuit be adjusted to increase the length of time it takes for the lock mechanism to be released after the power is switched off?

2.66 Whilst working on a television set an electronics technician accidentally touches a 10 000 µF capacitor that has charged to a voltage of 100 V. As a result of this the capacitor discharges across the finger of the technician causing a nasty burn.

(a) Calculate the energy that was stored in the capacitor.

(b) Calculate the temperature rise in the technician's finger assuming it has a specific heat capacity of 3 800 J kg^{-1}°C^{-1} and that the mass of tissue heated was 0·1 g.

2.67 Capacitors are used to provide short-term voltage back-up for memory chips in microcomputers. One such capacitor has a capacitance of 0·1 F and a voltage rating of 5·5 V. The leakage current from the capacitor is 100 µA.

Calculate how long it would take for the capacitor to become completely discharged assuming it discharges at a constant rate.

2.68 A circuit contains a resistor and capacitor in parallel. A signal which is a mixture of a.c. and d.c. is fed into the circuit. State which part of the signal, a.c. or d.c. will flow through the resistor. Justify your answer.

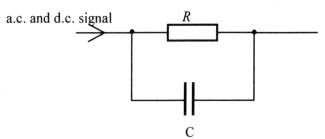

© P&N Publications

Analogue Electronics

Inverting amplifiers

2.69 An op-amp is set up for a school experiment using the circuit diagram shown below.

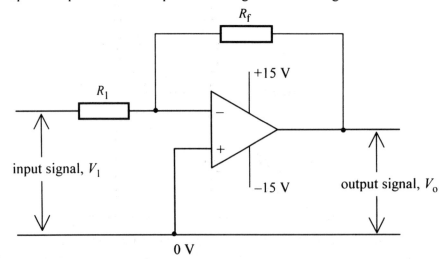

(a) The op-amp is set up in the inverting mode. State two changes that the op-amp in this mode makes to the input signal.

(b) If an op-amp is considered to be ideal what statements can be made about:

   (i) the size of current flowing into the op-amp input;

   (ii) the potential difference between the inverting and non–inverting inputs?

(c) A 5 mV signal is fed into the op-amp above. If R_1 has a value of 1 kΩ and R_f has a value of 100 kΩ, find the value of the output signal.

2.70 The op-amp shown in question **2.69** is now used with a range of resistor values and input signals. Calculate the missing values in order to complete the table below.

	Input signal, V_1	Output signal, V_o	Input resistor, R_1	Feedback resistor, R_f
(a)	0·5 V		10 kΩ	100 kΩ
(b)	20 mV		500 Ω	10 kΩ
(c)		–4 V	1 kΩ	100 kΩ
(d)	0·05 V	–5 V	1 kΩ	
(e)	5 mV	–10 V		1 MΩ
(f)	–20 mV		500 Ω	250 kΩ

2.71 A thermocouple is used to produce a small voltage as it is heated up. As its output is so small an op-amp is used to amplify it.

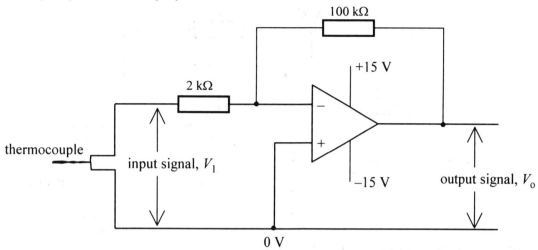

(a) If the op-amp is regarded as being 'ideal', what will be the voltage between the inverting and non-inverting inputs?

(b) (i) The thermocouple produces an input signal to the op-amp of 0.5×10^{-3} V. What will be the output voltage V_o?

(ii) The output voltage is fed to a standard voltmeter. However the voltage is not high enough to produce a satisfactory reading on the meter being used. What value of feedback resistor would be required to increase the output signal to 2·5 V?

2.72 The output voltage from an op-amp is plotted against the input voltage to produce the graph shown below.

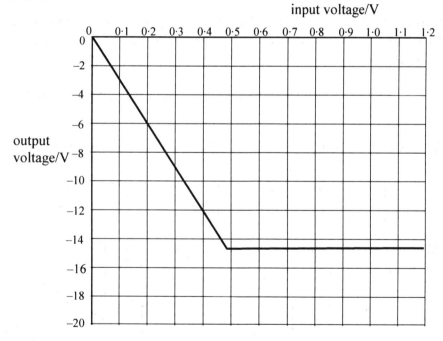

(a) (i) Find the gain of the amplifier.

(ii) If the input resistor has a value of 10 kΩ, find the value of the feedback resistor.

(b) Explain why the size of the output voltage reaches a maximum value even though the input voltage continues to increase.

2.73 An op-amp is connected to a sinusoidal waveform with a peak voltage of 0·5 V and a frequency of 50 Hz. The switch, S, is put to the closed position.

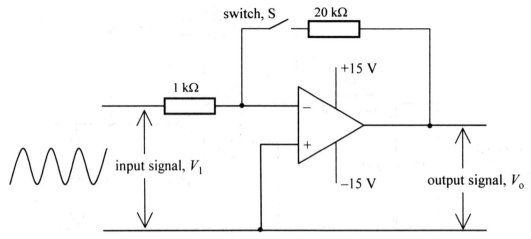

The graph below shows the input voltage against time.

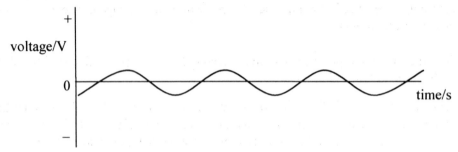

(a) (i) What will be the peak value of output from the op-amp?

(ii) Redraw the graph above and on the same set of axes, sketch the output voltage from the op-amp. Include a numerical value for the voltage.

(b) Redraw the input graph and sketch the output voltage which would be observed if resistor R_1 was replaced with one of 500 Ω resistance. Include a numerical value for the voltage.

(c) Describe the effect on the output from the op-amp if switch S was opened?

2.74 A pupil is experimenting with some op-amps and connects two in series as shown below.

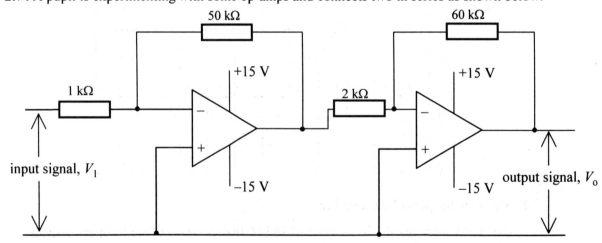

(a) Calculate the overall gain of the pair of op-amps.

(b) The input signal, V_1, is 2 mV. What will be the value of the output voltage V_o?

2.75 An op-amp is used to amplify a voltage. The circuit used for this is shown below.

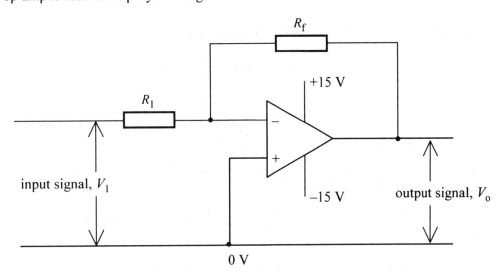

(a) The following resistors are placed into the circuit:
  R_1 5 kΩ
  R_f 100 kΩ
Calculate the value of V_o if V_1 is 0·1 V.

(b) The value of the resistors remains unchanged but the value of V_1 is now altered to –0·05 V. What will be the value of V_o now?

2.76 A pupil wishes to use an op-amp to produce a square wave output from an op-amp. Her circuit is shown below.

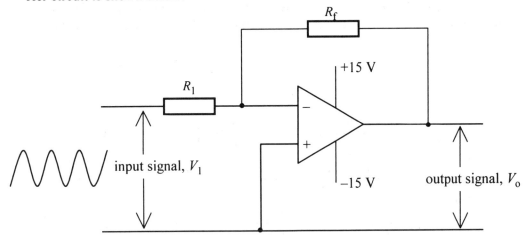

The signal she feeds into the op-amp is a sinusoidal waveform with a peak voltage of 0·5 V.

(a) Explain what is meant by the term saturation in respect to the output of the op-amp.

(b) (i) Describe how the circuit above could be used to convert the sinusoidal input into a square wave output.
  (ii) The circuit above is used with R_f equal to 1 MΩ and R_1 equal to 1 kΩ. Find the voltage the input must have reached for saturation to occur.

Differential amplifiers

2.77 An op-amp is set up as shown in the circuit diagram below.

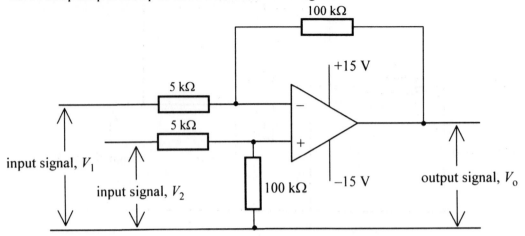

The op-amp has two inputs, V_1 and V_2. The voltage applied to V_1 is 0·4 V and the voltage applied to V_2 is 0·5 V.

(a) State the mode in which this op-amp is being used.

(b) (i) Calculate the output from this op-amp.

   (ii) What would be the output from the above circuit if the inputs V_1 and V_2 were reversed?

2.78 The op-amp shown below is used with a range of input resistors and voltages. The value of these are shown in the table. Use these values to find the value of the output voltage V_o.

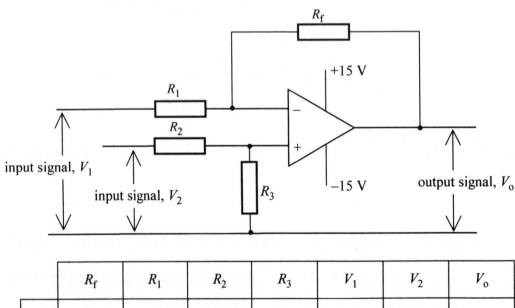

	R_f	R_1	R_2	R_3	V_1	V_2	V_o
(a)	100 kΩ	10 kΩ	10 kΩ	100 kΩ	0·5 V	0·6 V	
(b)	50 kΩ	1 kΩ	1 kΩ	50 kΩ	340 mV	380 mV	
(c)	20 kΩ	2 kΩ	2 kΩ	20 kΩ	2·35 V	2·05 V	
(d)	100 kΩ	10 kΩ	10 kΩ	100 kΩ	40 mV	−20 mV	

2.79 An op-amp is used to amplify the difference between two signals from a transducer. The circuit used is shown below.

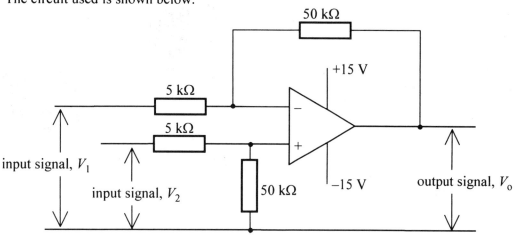

(a) State the equation used to calculate the output from an op-amp in the differential mode.

(b) What will be the output signal when the values of V_1 and V_2 are as follows:
   (i) $V_1 = 6{\cdot}85$ V and $V_2 = 6{\cdot}95$ V;
   (ii) $V_1 = 16{\cdot}40$ V and $V_2 = 15{\cdot}90$ V;
   (iii) $V_1 = 5{\cdot}3$ V and $V_2 = 7{\cdot}3$ V?

2.80 The op-amp shown below is designed to have a gain of 100.

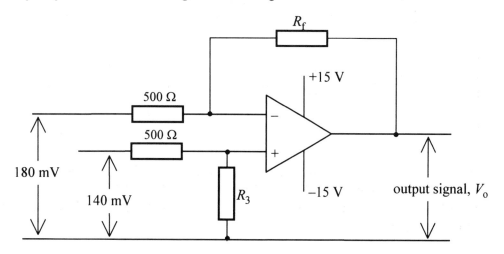

(a) What will be the value of R_f and R_3 if the op-amp is to meet its desired specification?

(b) What will be the output voltage when the input voltages are 180 mV and 140 mV as shown?

2.81 A hospital uses sensors attached to a patient's neck to monitor the blood supply to his head. The pulsing of blood through the artery to his head causes a potential difference between the two sensors. To ensure that other confusing signals such as mains signals are not amplified the sensors are attached to an op-amp in the differential mode.

Draw a suitable circuit for an op-amp in this mode. Indicate the position and value of resistors so that the op-amp gives a gain of 200.

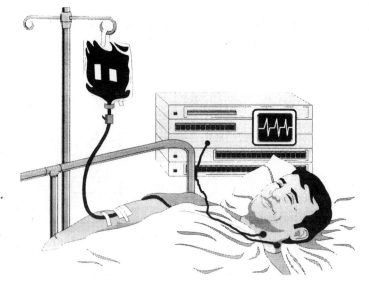

2.82 A light dependent resistor is used in a Wheatstone bridge circuit so that small changes in light levels can be accurately measured during an experiment. It is decided to amplify the output from the bridge circuit using an op-amp in the differential mode.

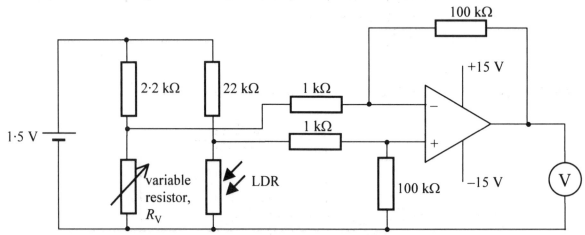

(a) The LDR is placed in the lighting conditions at which it is desired to have zero output from the voltmeter. At this light level the resistance of the LDR is 10 kΩ. To what value of resistance will the variable resistor, R_V, have to be set to obtain 0 V from the output of the op-amp?

(b) The light level falling on the LDR now decreases and its resistance rises. What is the potential difference between the inputs to the op-amp if its output is 1·8 V?

(c) The pupil now tries to use this circuit to measure absolute light level and balances the bridge in complete darkness. When he tries to measure light level however, the voltmeter reading rises to a fixed level which does not increase as the light falling on the LDR increases. Explain this observation.

2.83 An op-amp receives two inputs in the form of square–wave pulses. The op-amp circuit and the two inputs are shown below.

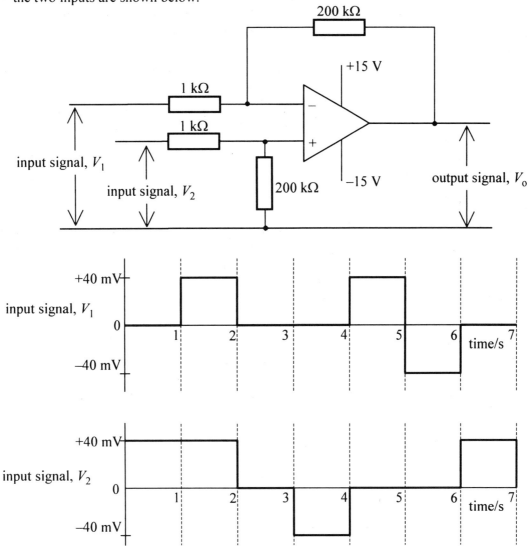

(a) (i) What is the mode in which the op-amp is working?

  (ii) State an equation for the output voltage V_o in terms of the input voltages V_1 and V_2.

(b) Calculate the gain of the amplifier.

(c) Draw a graph to show how the output V_o varies over the time interval 0 to 7 s given that the inputs are as shown in the graphs above.

2.84 A yogurt maker contains a low power heating element which is permanently switched on in order to keep the yogurt mixture warm. An enterprising pupil decides to build an electronic circuit which will switch on the heater if the temperature drops too low and then switch it off again as the temperature rises. Her circuit design is shown below.

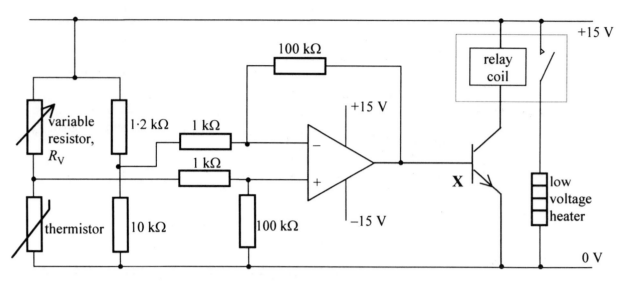

The resistance of the thermistor **decreases** as its temperature **increases**. Resistor R_V is used to initially balance the bridge circuit at the desired yogurt temperature.

(a) (i) What will be the resistance of the thermistor if the variable resistor has to be set to a value of 7·5 kΩ to obtain a balanced bridge?

(ii) What will be the output voltage from the op-amp when the bridge is balanced?

(b) The temperature of the yogurt begins to fall. What effect has this on the voltage at:

(i) the inverting input to the op-amp;

(ii) the non-inverting input to the op-amp?

(c) (i) What is the name of the component labelled **X**?

(ii) Explain how the fall in temperature is able to switch on the electric heater.

(d) The pupil also attempts to build a simple temperature indicator which illuminates either a green or red LED depending upon whether the temperature of the yogurt is too high or too low. The circuit for this is shown below.

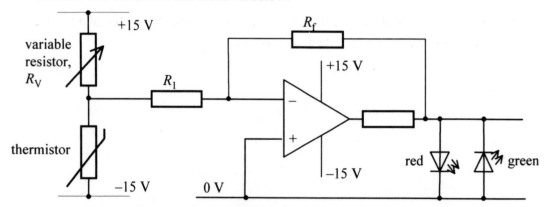

The variable resistor is adjusted until the input voltage to the op-amp is zero.
Which LED will illuminate as the temperature of the yogurt rises? Explain your answer.

Unit 3—Radiation and Matter

Waves

Wave characteristics

3.1 A sound wave has a frequency of 2 kHz. What is the period of the wave?

3.2 The pendulum on a clock oscillates with a period of 0·8 s. What is the frequency of its swing?

3.3 A microwave oven produces microwaves with a wavelength of 0·03 m in air.

   (*a*) Calculate the frequency of these microwaves.

   (*b*) Find the period of the microwaves in air.

3.4 A tuning fork vibrates at a frequency of 512 Hz.

   (*a*) What will be the frequency of the sound waves emitted by the fork?

   (*b*) The sound waves produced by two tuning forks are fed into an oscilloscope. Which of the two traces shown below comes form the fork which is producing the greatest amount of energy? Explain your answer.

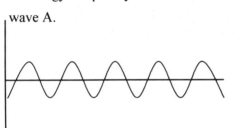
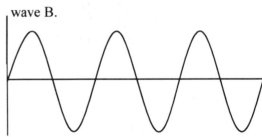

Interference

3.5 A pupil comes across the following phrases in her Higher Physics notes. Explain carefully, with the aid of sketches, what **each** one means:
   (i) waves that are *in phase;*
   (ii) waves that are *out of phase;*
   (iii) *coherent* waves.

3.6 A teacher uses a large tray of water to demonstrate the interference of waves. Two 'dippers' vibrate in and out of the water to produce the wave pattern shown opposite. Each line on the diagram represents a wave crest and each dotted line a wave trough.

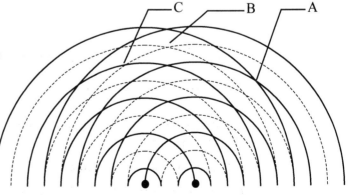

   (*a*) What type of interference is occurring at point A, B and C?

   (*b*) It is important for this experiment that the waves produced are coherent. Explain how this could be achieved.

3.7 An experiment is set up to demonstrate the interference of light. A light bulb is viewed through a glass slide coated with black paint. Two narrow slits, close together, are cut through the paint. Red and blue clear plastic filters are available to place over the bulb.

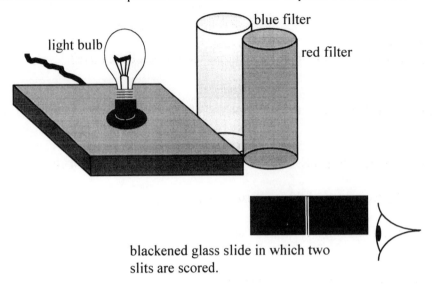

blackened glass slide in which two slits are scored.

(a) Describe how this experiment is able to provide coherent light sources.

(b) The red plastic filter is placed over the light bulb and it switched on. The viewer sees the following pattern through the slits on the glass slide.

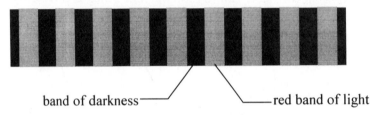

band of darkness ———— red band of light

Explain what is happening at;
  (i) the red band;
  (ii) the dark band.

(c) The red filter is now removed and replaced with the blue filter. The following pattern is now observed.

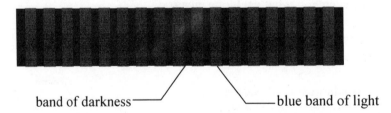

band of darkness ———— blue band of light

Suggest a reason for the different spacing of the bands.

(d) The blue filter is now removed. Describe what would now be seen through the slits.

(e) The red filter is now replaced over the light so that the pattern observed through the slits is as shown in part (b) of this question. Describe and explain any changes in this pattern if:
  (i) the brightness of the lamp is reduced;
  (ii) one of the slits on the slide is covered over.

3.8 (a) The following effects are all characteristic behaviours of a wave motion. Describe an example which illustrates each one. You may use any type of wave motion (e.g. radio waves, water waves, light waves, sound waves etc.):

  (i) reflection;

  (ii) refraction;

  (iii) diffraction;

  (iv) interference.

(b) Which of the above effects is a test for a wave?

3.9 A microwave transmitter is placed behind metal plates as shown below. The detector, attached to a voltmeter to indicate the strength of the received signal, is placed in front of the slits.

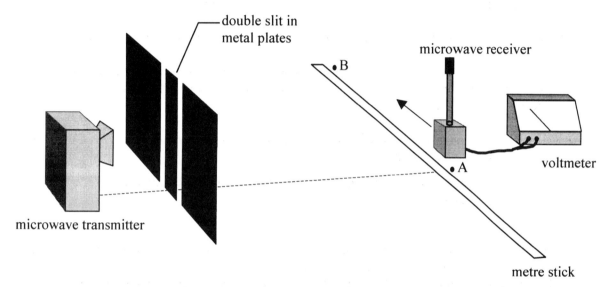

(a) This experiment uses only a single microwave source behind two slits to provide two sources of waves. Why is this done?

(b) (i) The microwave receiver is placed at point A which is an equal distance from each of the slits. Describe the reading on the voltmeter.

  (ii) The receiver is now moved along the metre stick towards point B. Describe what would happen to the reading on the voltmeter and provide an explanation for this.

(c) A pupil remembers his teacher describing the effect of path difference on the voltmeter reading.

  (i) What is mean by the expression *path difference*?

  (ii) What would the voltmeter indicate where the path difference is:

    A two whole wavelengths;

    B three whole wavelengths;

    C four and a half wavelengths?

(d) At one point along the metre stick the receiver is placed 38·5 cm from one slit and 47·5 cm from the other. If the wavelength of the microwaves being used is 3 cm, what would be observed on the voltmeter?

© P&N Publications

3.10 Two loudspeakers are connected to a signal generator which produces a steady note with a frequency of 3400 Hz.

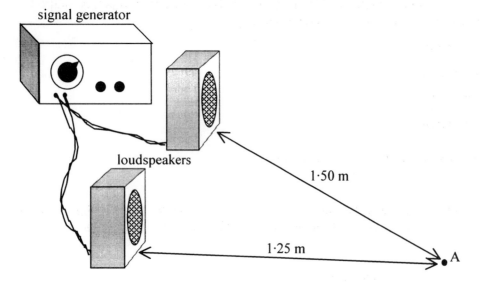

(a) Calculate the wavelength of the sound waves being produced by the loudspeakers.

(b) A microphone is placed at position A which is 1·25 m from one loudspeaker and 1·50 m from the other. State, providing evidence for your answer, whether constructive or destructive interference will be found at this point.

(c) (i) The frequency of the signal is now doubled. What effect would this have on the type of interference found at A?

  (ii) What would happen to the signal at A if one of the loudspeakers were now to be disconnected?

3.11 Two loudspeakers are connected to a signal generator in order to produce two coherent sources of sound. The signal generator produces a signal with a wavelength of 0·3 m. A listener stands at the central maximum where she hears a loud signal. She then walks to the side until she reaches the 3rd order maximum where she also hears a loud signal.

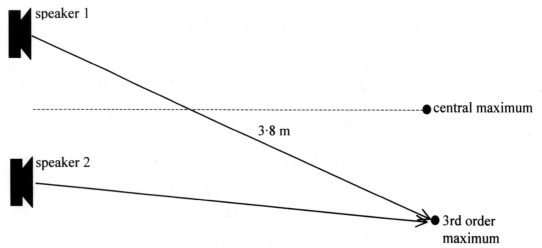

If the distance between speaker 1 and the 3rd order maximum is 3·8 m, find the distance between speaker 2 and the 3rd order maximum.

3.12 A school experiment can be used to demonstrate interference using a single source of sound. A loudspeaker is situated close to a wall and sound waves allowed to reflect from this to a listener who is situated at A as shown below. The wavelength of the sound wave being emitted is 20 cm.

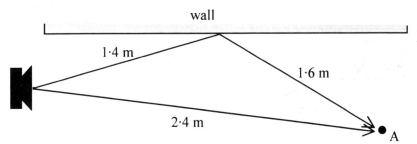

(a) Explain how interference is produced even though there is only one source of waves.

(b) Describe what would be heard at position A giving a reason for your answer.

(c) The experiment is carried out inside the school physics classroom and also outside in the open. The interference effects are not nearly as clear when the experiment is carried out in the classroom. Suggest a reason for this.

3.13 A microwave transmitter is aimed at a metal plate placed directly in front of it. A detector connected to a voltmeter is placed between the plate and transmitter to indicate the strength of signal at different positions along the metre stick.

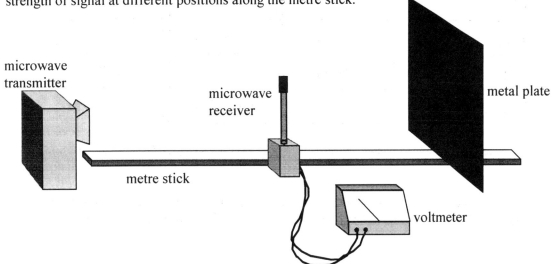

The microwave receiver is placed approximately half-way between the metal plate and transmitter in such a position that it picks up a maximum signal.

(a) The metal plate is moved slowly backwards. A pupil observes the voltmeter readings and writes the following note. *"When moved backwards the voltmeter reading increased to a maximum then fell to almost zero as follows: maximum, minimum, maximum, minimum, maximum minimum, maximum."* Explain the pupil's observation in terms of the interference of microwaves.

(b) During the experiment the reflector was moved back a total distance of 4·2 cm.

(i) What is the wavelength of the microwaves?

(ii) What is the frequency of the microwaves?

(c) The pupil also noticed that as he moved the reflector back the voltmeter reading was slightly less at each successive maximum. Suggest a reason for this observation.

Diffraction Gratings

3.14 A diffraction grating is placed in front of a laser which provides a monochromatic light source. A screen is placed a few metres in front of the grating.

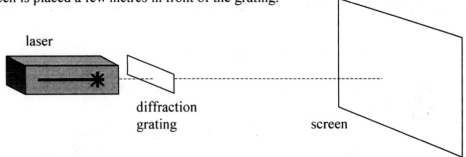

(a) Explain what is meant by a *monochromatic* light source.

(b) A single red dot is seen on the screen before the grating is in place. What would be observed on the screen when the grating is placed in front of the laser beam?

3.15 (a) Use the formula $n\lambda = d\sin\theta$ to complete the missing entries in the following table.

	Order of fringe	Wavelength of light	Distance between lines on grating	Angle to normal
(i)	1		$2 \cdot 3 \times 10^{-6}$ m	15°
(ii)	4	550 nm	5×10^{-6} m	
(iii)	3	400 nm		29°
(iv)	2	700 nm	1×10^{-5} m	

(b) What colour of light was used in part (ii), (iii) and (iv) of part (a) of this question?

3.16 A laser beam is directed at a diffraction grating which has 300 lines per mm. Calculate the deviation of the 3rd order maximum if the wavelength of the laser light is 514 nm.

3.17 A tungsten filament lamp provides a source of white light. A blue filter is placed in front of the lamp so that a beam of light with a wavelength of 450 nm is focused onto a diffraction grating. Calculate the number of lines per mm on the grating if the deviation of the 1st order maximum is 6·5° from the centre.

3.18 A sodium vapour lamp is used to produce light with a wavelength of 589×10^{-9} m which is then directed at a diffraction grating with 200 lines per mm. One of the fringes was observed to have a deviation of 20·7° from the centre. Which order of fringe was being examined?

3.19 Although light is diffracted as it passes through a diffraction grating, the fringes produced on the screen are the result of another wave characteristic. State the wave characteristic responsible for these fringes.

3.20 Light from a white light source is shone onto a grating with 300 lines per mm. The pattern observed on the screen is shown below.

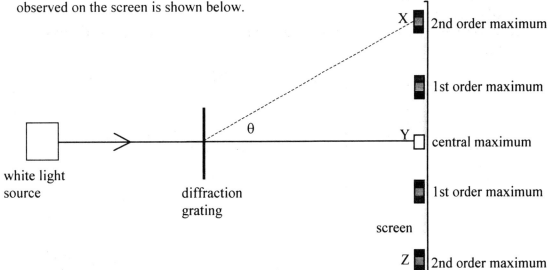

(a) Describe the appearance of the maxima found at:

(i) Y;

(ii) Z.

(b) State the approximate wavelength of the colour of light found nearest the central maximum in the fringe at Z.

(c) The light found at position X has a wavelength of 500×10^{-9} m. Find the angle θ that this ray of light makes with the normal.

3.21 A laser is fired through a diffraction grating with 100 lines per millimetre. The resulting pattern appears on a screen placed 2 m in front of the grating. The diagram below shows the experimental set–up. For clarity only the central maximum and those to its right are shown.

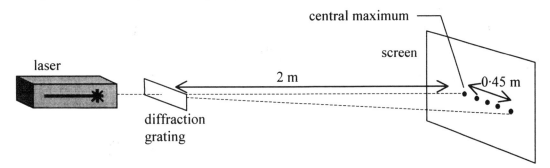

(a) Using information obtained from the diagram, calculate the wavelength of the light emitted by the laser.

(b) What would be the effect on the appearance of the pattern on the screen if:

(i) the diffraction grating was replaced with one with 200 lines per millimetre;

(ii) the distance between the grating and the screen was increased?

(c) (i) The laser is replaced with a white light source. Describe the appearance of the pattern observed on the screen.

(ii) A prism can be used to split a light source into its component wavelengths. State **two** ways in which the spectrum from a prism is different from that produced by a diffraction grating.

© P&N Publications

Refraction of Light

Refractive index of light

3.22 Calculate the refractive index of the transparent material used in each of the following situations.

(a)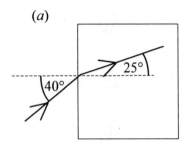

(b)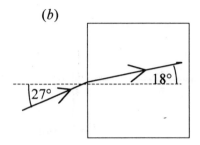

(c)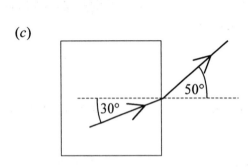

(d)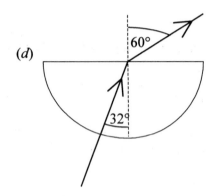

3.23 Find the value of the unknown angle θ in each of the following examples.

(a)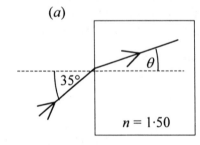

(b)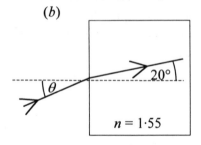

(c)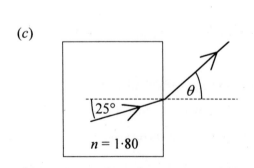

(d)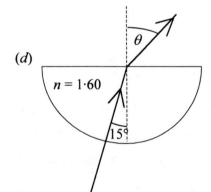

3.24 Find the refractive index of the glass block shown below.

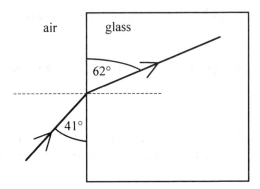

3.25 A pupil is asked to find the relationship between the angle an incident ray makes on a glass block and the angle at which the ray is refracted within the glass block. A ray box is used with a red filter placed in front of it so that only red light enters the glass block.

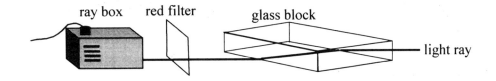

The angle between the incident ray and the normal θ_1, was measured and also the angle between the refracted ray and the normal θ_2. The pupil then used these to find the sine value for each angle.

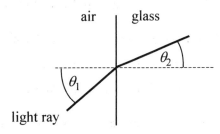

A table of the pupil's results is shown below.

$\sin \theta_1$	0·174	0·342	0·5	0·643	0·766
$\sin \theta_2$	0·112	0·221	0·323	0·415	0·494

(a) Plot a graph of the pupil's results.

(b) Use the graph plotted in part (a) to determine a value for the refractive index of the glass block.

(c) The red filter is replaced with a blue one and it is noticed that the angle of refraction changes from those obtained with the red filter. Explain this observation.

3.26 A glass block has a refractive index of 1·58. What will be the angle of the refracted light in the block if the incident light makes an angle of 34° with the normal?

3.27 Light with a wavelength of 400 nm falls on a glass block. What will be the wavelength of light within the block if it has a refractive index of 1·50?

3.28 (a) What is the velocity of light in air?

(b) What will be the velocity of light within a lens made of glass with a refractive index of 1·48?

(c) If the light being used has a frequency of 6×10^{14} Hz in air, what will be its frequency within the lens?

3.29 A glass prism is used to split a beam of white light into its component colours. A diagram of the prism is shown below. The ray B, makes an angle of 18·8° with the normal and the angle between ray A and ray B is 0·4°.

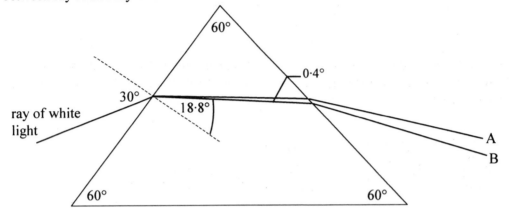

(a) What colour of light will be found at positions A and B?

(b) Through calculation, find the refractive index of the glass for:
   (i) light of the wavelength found at position A;
   (ii) light of the wavelength found at position B.

(c) State what happens to the following as the light leaves the prism:
   (i) its frequency;
   (ii) its wavelength;
   (iii) its velocity.

3.30 A layer of ice rests on a pane of glass. The following information is known about the refractive index of each relative to air.
   ice − 1·31
   glass − 1·51
By considering the diagram opposite, decide which substance is A and which B.

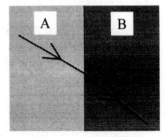

Total internal reflection

3.31 A ray of light is shone into a semi-circular glass block as shown below.

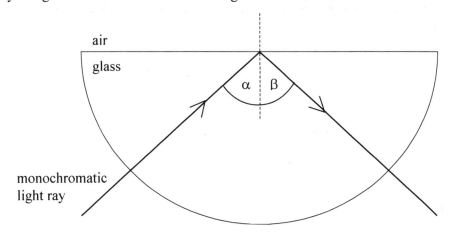

The light ray is observed to be reflected back from the face of the glass block and no light exits into the air. A textbook states that *"total internal reflection occurs when the angle of incidence within the glass block is above the critical angle."*

(a) Explain what is meant by:

   (i) total internal reflection;

   (ii) the critical angle.

(b) State the relationship between the angle α and the angle β?

(c) The ray of light is now rotated so that the ray entering the block exits along the face of the block as shown below.

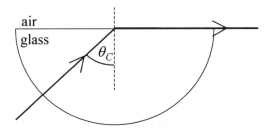

By considering the path of the ray through the block, derive the equation

$$\sin\theta_C = \frac{1}{n}$$

where θ_C is the critical angle.

3.32 A ray of light emerges from a glass block into the air at an angle of 90° to the normal. Find the refractive index of the glass if the angle between the ray and the normal within the block was 42°.

3.33 Find the critical angle for water if it has a refractive index of 1·33.

3.34 A car speedometer uses plastic rods to direct light to different parts of the display by utilising the property of total internal reflection. The plastic has a refractive index of 1·47. Find if the ray of light in the diagram below will be totally internally reflected and provide evidence for your conclusion.

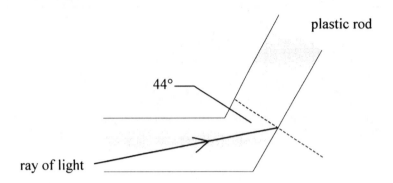

3.35 Poor quality optical lenses can suffer from a fault which causes different colours of light to focus at slightly different focal points. A diagram of part of the lens is shown below.

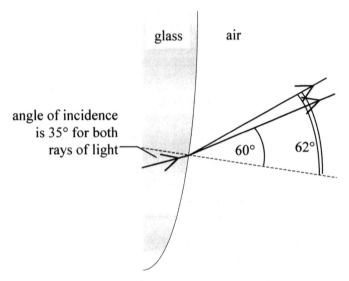

Both colours of light have an angle of incidence of 35° but light with a wavelength of 450 nm is refracted at 60° and light with a wavelength of 700 nm is refracted at 62°.

(a) Calculate the refractive index of the glass for:

   (i) light with a wavelength of 450 nm;

   (ii) light with a wavelength of 700 nm.

(b) What would be the critical angle for this glass for:

   (i) light with a wavelength of 450 nm;

   (ii) light with a wavelength of 700 nm?

(c) If this lens were to be used in a simple magnifying glass how would the image appear compared to that produced by a high quality lens?

3.36 A popular party trick is to place a pound coin in the base of an opaque cup and place your eye so that it is just out of the line of sight and cannot be seen for the rim of the cup.
When lemonade is poured into the cup the coin becomes visible.

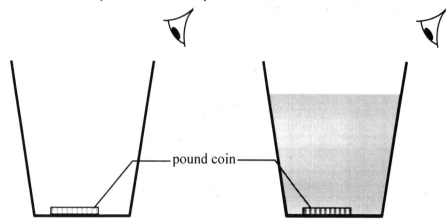

In empty cup the coin is hidden behind the rim of the cup.

When cup is filled with lemonade the coin becomes visible.

(a) Explain why the coin is visible in the cup containing the lemonade but not in the empty cup even although the viewer's eye has not moved. Include a diagram of the cup to help with your explanation.

(b) The lemonade has a refractive index of 1·35. Above what angle will it be impossible for a ray of light from the coin to escape from the lemonade?

Optoelectronics

Intensity of radiation

3.37 Find the missing entries in the following table.

	Intensity	Power	Area
(a)		1 W	1 m²
(b)		100 W	8 m²
(c)	3 W m⁻²	500 mW	
(d)	2·4 W m⁻²		200 cm²
(e)	150 mW m⁻²	2 W	

3.38 A projector uses a 300 W bulb and projects its light onto a screen measuring 2 m by 3 m. What will be the light intensity at the screen assuming there is no light loss?

3.39 A table lamp reflects all of its light onto the table on which it stands. The light intensity at the table top is 200 W m⁻²? What will be the area of table illuminated if the lamp contains a 40 W bulb?

3.40 Find the missing entries in the following table.

	Light Intensity I_1	Light Intensity I_2	Distance d_1	Distance d_2
(a)		40 mW m⁻²	0·5 m	2 m
(b)	10 W m⁻²		2 m	4 m
(c)	0·8 W m⁻²	0·05 W m⁻²	1 m	
(d)	2·56 W m⁻²	0·02 W m⁻²		2 m
(e)	2 W m⁻²		2 m	0·25 m

3.41 A householder buys an outdoor light to illuminate her garden at night. She fits a 100 W light bulb but is surprised to find that the garden is only poorly lit compared to a room fitted with an identical bulb. Explain why the bulb can light a small room well but a large garden is poorly lit in comparison.

© P&N Publications

3.42 A solar cell is placed at a distance of 20 cm from a light source in an otherwise dark room. The output from the cell is 800 mV. The cell is now moved to a distance of 80 cm from the source. Assuming the light output from the cell is proportional to the light intensity on it, what will be its new output voltage?

3.43 A photographic light meter indicates a light intensity of 4 W m^{-2} at a distance of 2·0 m from a light source. What separation from the light source would be required to produce a light intensity of 0·25 W m^{-2}?

3.44 An experiment is set up in the school dark room to measure how light intensity varies with distance. The apparatus used and the results obtained are shown below.

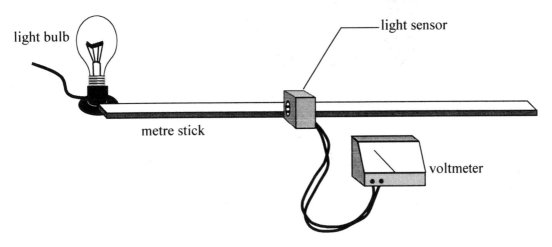

Results

Distance between bulb and sensor (m)	0·1	0·2	0·3	0·4	0·5	0·6
Voltmeter reading (mV)	402	99	44	25	16	11

The distance between the light bulb and the light sensor is varied and the voltmeter reading and distance recorded.

(a) (i) What assumption has to be made about the voltage output from the sensor at various light levels?

  (ii) Why must the experiment be performed in a dark room?

(b) Show the relationship between distance and light intensity using the results obtained by the pupil.

(c) The light sensor is now moved to a distance of 1 m from the lamp. Predict what the voltage reading would be at that distance.

Photoelectric emission

3.45 Amy and Adil carry out an experiment at school one day where they use a device known as a gold leaf electroscope along with a range of different light sources.

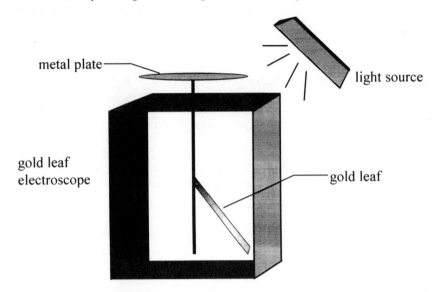

(a) The purpose of the pupils' experiment is to investigate the process of photoelectric emission. Explain what is meant by *photoelectric emission*.

(b) The experiment begins with Amy shining a range of different light sources onto the metal plate of a negatively charged electroscope. If the leaf of the electroscope falls it is an indication that the electroscope has discharged. What will she observe if she uses the following light sources with a metal plate made of zinc:

   (i) a tungsten lamp producing visible light;

   (ii) an ultraviolet lamp;

   (iii) a very bright halogen lamp producing white light?

(c) Adil suggests that they should try using a plate made of steel. They replace the zinc plate by a steel one and recharge the electroscope negatively. State clearly which of the first three experiments (i), (ii) or (iii) will produce a **different** result. Explain the reason for this difference.

3.46 The graph opposite shows how a photoelectric current varies with the frequency of incident radiation on a particular metal surface.

(a) What is a *photon*?

(b) Explain the significance of the point marked f_o on the frequency axis.

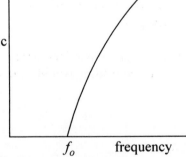

(c) (i) Radiation is used which has a frequency less than f_o. What effect will increasing the **intensity** of this radiation have on the photoelectric current?

   (ii) Radiation above the frequency of f_o is now used. What effect will increasing the intensity of the radiation have on the photoelectric current?

3.47 What is the energy of a photon of ultraviolet light if the frequency of the light is 8.6×10^{14} Hz?

3.48 A light source emits a photon with 3.3×10^{-19} J of energy. What is the frequency of the light source?

3.49 The work function of a metal is 6.4×10^{-19} J.

(a) Explain what is meant by the term 'work function'.

(b) Light with a wavelength of 250 nm is shone onto the metal surface.
   (i) What is the frequency of the light?
   (ii) Find whether or not the photons of this light will cause the photoelectric effect to take place.

(c) The light source is now replaced with a light source which produces light with a frequency of 1.5×10^{15} Hz.
   (i) The photons from this source contain more energy than is required to release the electrons. How much extra energy is available after the electron has been released?
   (ii) Into what energy type will this extra energy be converted?

3.50 An electron is released from the surface of a metal plate which has a work function of 4.5×10^{-19} J. What frequency of light is required to just release an electron from this metal?

3.51 Light falls on a metal plate and electrons are ejected with a maximum kinetic energy of 1.6×10^{-19} J. Calculate the work function of the metal if the light shining on the plate has a frequency of 7.5×10^{14} Hz.

3.52 A device known as a photoelectric cell makes use of the photoelectric effect to measure light levels. The construction of a typical photoelectric cell is shown below.

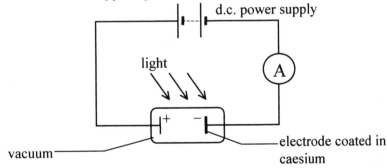

(a) The caesium electrode will produce a current when light with a wavelength above 12 μm strikes it. What is the work function of the caesium?

(b) (i) Why must the tube be a vacuum before a current will flow in the circuit?
   (ii) What effect would reversing the power supply have on the operation of the photocell?

(c) Explain how increasing the intensity of light falling on the caesium coated electrode produces a greater reading on the ammeter.

3.53 A metal has a work function of $1·5 \times 10^{-20}$ J.

  (a) Find the kinetic energy of an ejected electron if a photon striking the metal has a frequency of 3×10^{13} Hz.

  (b) What will be the maximum possible velocity of the ejected electrons?

3.54 2×10^{19} photons of light with a frequency of 3×10^{14} Hz fall on each square metre of a metal plate. Calculate the intensity of light on the plate.

3.55 A lamp emits monochromatic light with a frequency of $7·5 \times 10^{14}$ Hz.

  (a) What is the energy of one photon from the lamp?

  (b) Light from the lamp illuminates a photocell at an intensity of 2 W m^{-2}. How many photons hit the photocell each second if the cell has an area of 5×10^{-5} m^2?

3.56 Integrated circuits called EPROMs have a small window on their surface which allows ultraviolet light to be shone onto the surface of the internal circuitry.

This allows the EPROM to be reprogrammed with new information. Special machines are used to carry out the erasing process and they use special ultraviolet tubes. The specification for one of these tubes is given below.

Ultraviolet wavelength	253·7 nm
Ultraviolet intensity	0·6 μW m^{-2}
Erasing area	24×10^{-3} m^2

  (a) Calculate the photon energy of the ultraviolet source.

  (b) How many photons are produced by the source each second?

  (c) As the ultraviolet tube ages the brightness of the tube decreases. What effect will this have on the photon energy of the radiation produced by the lamp? Give reasons for your answer.

Emission and absorption spectra

3.57 The diagram below shows the line spectra produced by a hydrogen gas discharge tube when viewed through a spectroscope.

  (a) Draw a diagram to show the energy levels of a hydrogen atom. Label the ground level and the excited levels clearly. (Energy values are not required).

  (b) Describe what happens when an electron makes a transition from an excited energy level to an energy level which is less excited.

3.58 The energy levels diagram for an atom is shown below.

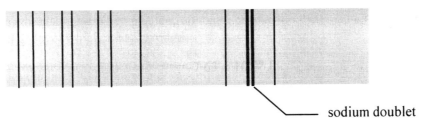

(a) How many lines will be observed in the line spectrum of this atom?

(b) Find the wavelength of the spectral line which has:

(i) the shortest wavelength;

(ii) the longest wavelength.

3.59 A sodium discharge tube is used to produce a bright orange light. The line emission spectrum contains two intense yellow lines called the sodium doublet.

The wavelengths of these lines are 589·0 nm and 589·6 nm.

(a) Explain why the doublet lines are much brighter than other lines in the sodium spectrum.

(b) Show that the photon energy associated with each of the doublet lines is almost identical.

3.60 A spectroscope is pointed firstly at a tungsten lamp producing white light and then at a helium discharge tube.

Describe what would be seen for each of these sources and account for any differences.

3.61 An experiment is set up in a school laboratory to demonstrate an absorption spectrum and the apparatus for this is shown below. A stick of sodium salts is put into the bunsen flame to produce a coloured flame

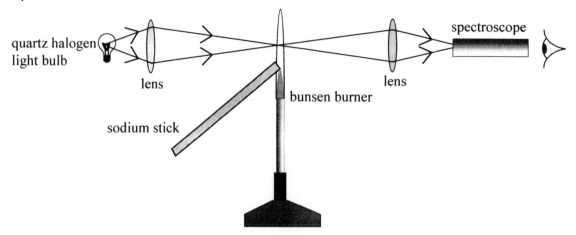

The quartz halogen light bulb produces a very bright white light and this is focused onto the bunsen flame. The light is then focused onto a spectrometer so that the spectrum from the flame can be observed.

(a) Describe what is seen through the spectroscope eyepiece when:

(i) the quartz halogen lamp only is on;

(ii) the sodium stick only is in the bunsen flame;

(iii) both the quartz halogen lamp is on **and** the sodium stick is placed in the bunsen flame.

(b) The spectrum is observed in (a) (iii) is known as an *absorption spectrum*. Explain how this absorption spectrum is produced.

(c) One of the lines where light is absorbed occurs at a wavelength of 595 nm. What is the energy associated with photons at this frequency?

(d) How would the appearance of the absorption spectrum differ if the sodium stick were to be replaced by a different element such as lithium? Explain your answer.

3.62 Absorption spectrometers enable identification of elements through the production of an absorption spectrum. Light from a white light source is directed onto a prism which splits the light into its constituent wavelengths. These are passed through the sample to be analysed to produce an absorption spectrum.

   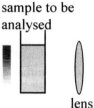

(a) (i) Explain how the dark lines are produced on the spectrum at the detector.

(ii) How does the presence of these lines enable elements in the sample to be identified?

(b) What device other than a prism could be used to produce a spectrum in the spectrometer?

3.63 Scientists examining the light from the Sun and other stars have passed the light through a spectrometer and noticed the presence of absorption lines in the spectrum.

(a) Explain why these lines appear on the spectrum.

(b) One of these lines appears at a wavelength of 656 nm.

   (i) Calculate the photon energy associated with this line.

   (ii) What colour of light would have been present at this line?

Lasers

3.64 Laser is a word produced from the first letter of the five words which describe the function of a laser. What does L.A.S.E.R. stand for?

3.65 A diagrammatic view of a helium-neon laser is shown below.

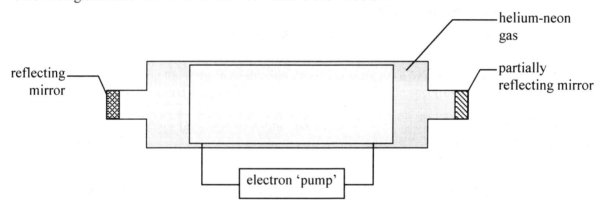

(a) (i) The laser produces light by the *'stimulated emission'* of photons. Explain how the emission of photons is stimulated.

   (ii) What is the difference between *'stimulated emission'* and *'spontaneous emission'*?

   (iii) What is the property of the photons produced by stimulated emission which creates a laser beam rather than just a beam of light?

(b) At the end of the laser tube there is a reflecting mirror and a partially reflecting mirror.

   (i) Through which of these mirrors is the laser beam emitted?

   (ii) Explain the role of the mirrors in the production of the laser beam.

(c) The laser beam is different from a light beam produced by an ordinary light source. State **two** ways in which it is different.

3.66 A carbon dioxide laser contains carbon dioxide gas. What will be the wavelength of the photons from this laser if they have an energy of $2 \cdot 1 \times 10^{-20}$ J?

3.67 A 1 mW helium–neon laser produces a continuous laser beam with a wavelength of 633×10^{-9} m.

(a) Calculate the energy of a single photon from the laser beam.

(b) The laser beam strikes a target of 2 mm diameter.

(i) Find the intensity of the laser beam at the target.

(ii) How many photons strike the target each second?

(c) Explain why the laser is more hazardous if looked at directly than a light bulb which may be many times more powerful.

3.68 A ruby laser produces a very short pulse of light lasting for $1 \cdot 2 \times 10^{-16}$ s. The energy of each photon of the laser beam is $2 \cdot 87 \times 10^{-19}$ J.

(a) (i) The ruby laser beam is rated at 2 W. How much energy is deposited on a target with a single pulse of the laser?

(ii) What assumptions must be made in calculating the above?

(b) What happens to the light energy when the laser light is absorbed by the target?

Semiconductors

3.69 (a) State the difference between conductor, insulator and semiconductor materials and give an example of each.

(b) Semiconductors can be of either n-type or p-type. What are the majority charge carriers in:

(i) n-type;

(ii) p-type?

(c) The diagram below represents the atoms in a semiconductor material made up of germanium atoms doped with arsenic.

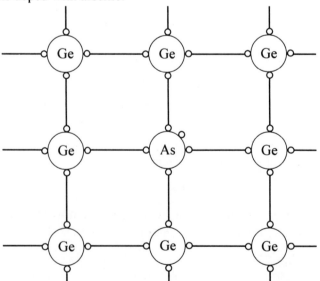

(i) Is the semiconductor material in the diagram n-type or p-type?

(ii) What is the overall charge on the semiconductor?

3.70 An electronic device consists of a block of p-type material and n-type material joined together.

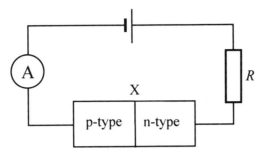

(a) What name is given to the device labelled, X?

(b) (i) In the diagram above, is the p-n junction forward or reverse biased?

(ii) State whether the ammeter will give a reading or not.

(c) (i) Explain why the p-n junction does not conduct when reverse biased.

(ii) Why does the p-n junction conduct when forward biased?

3.71 A digital display uses seven segment LED displays as shown opposite.

Each segment of the display consists of a single LED which can be illuminated on its own or with other segments.

(a) Describe what occurs at the p-n junction of the LED when it is forward biased.

(b) (i) The LED emits light with a wavelength of 655 nm. Calculate the energy of one emitted photon.

(ii) In reality, not all the energy produced by the LED is converted into light. In what form is the lost energy?

(iii) A particular LED has a recombination energy of $3 \cdot 98 \times 10^{-19}$ J. What colour of light does the LED emit?

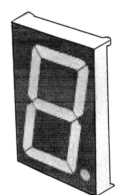

3.72 Photodiodes can be used in a range of circuit applications.

(a) Name **two** modes in which photodiodes operate.

(b) What is the mode called where the photodiode:

(i) supplies power to a load;

(ii) acts as a light sensor?

(c) (i) In one mode of operation there are electron-hole pairs created which produce an e.m.f. across the p-n junction of the photodiode. Where does the energy come from to cause this separation?

(ii) Why does increasing the light intensity falling on the photodiode produce a larger e.m.f?

3.73 A pupil sets up a photodiode in the following circuit.

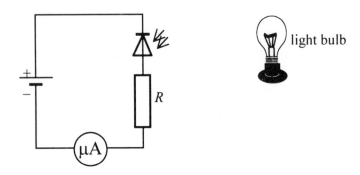

(a) (i) In what mode is the photodiode being used?

(ii) Suggest a possible application for a circuit of this type.

(b) The reading on the microammeter is 100 µA when the light bulb is placed 10 cm from the photodiode. What will the microammeter read when the light bulb is moved to 80 cm from the photodiode?

(c) A pupil experiments with the transmission of infra red from a LED. He connects the LED to a supply oscillating at a high frequency. What property of the photodiode makes it particularly suitable as a receiver for the pulsed light?

3.74 The circuit symbol shown below is for an n-channel MOSFET, a type of transistor.

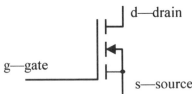

(a) State **one** use of a MOSFET in an electronic circuit.

(b) To which of the three connections shown is a positive voltage applied in order to make the MOSFET operate?

3.75 A circuit is set up incorporating a MOSFET as shown below. The MOSFET is used to switch on the lamp when the light level falls below a certain value.

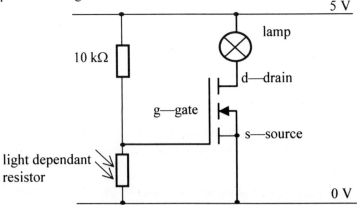

(a) The light dependent resistor has a resistance of 40 kΩ in the dark. Calculate the voltage present at the gate under these conditions.

(b) Explain fully how the decrease in light level causes the lamp to be turned on.

3.76 The diagram below shows a section through a typical MOSFET.

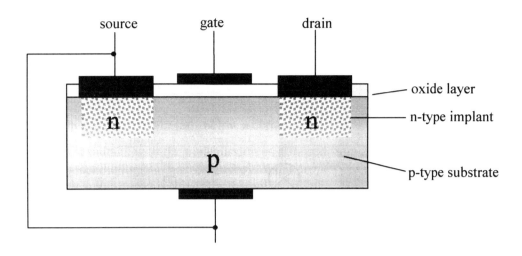

(a) A positive voltage is applied to the gate of the MOSFET. State whether this turns the MOSFET on or off.

(b) Whilst the gate is connected to a positive voltage, the source and drain are connected to a negative voltage. Explain the effect this has on current flow through the MOSFET.

Nuclear Reactions

Nature of radiation

3.77 Rutherford's alpha particle scattering experiment used the apparatus shown in the simplified diagram shown below.

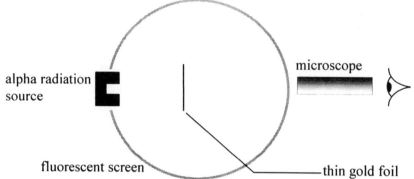

(a) (i) What was the observer looking for when viewing the fluorescent screen through the microscope?

   (ii) What was the expected outcome of firing alpha particles at very thin gold foil?

(b) Rutherford discovered that the majority of alpha particles passed through the foil. Many alpha particles were deflected when they hit the gold foil however and that some even bounced back in the direction in which they had come. State **two** conclusions Rutherford was able to draw from these observations.

(c) The apparatus shown above was placed in a vacuum to perform the experiment. Why was a vacuum necessary for this experiment?

3.78 A pupil sees the following symbol on a periodic table.

(a) How many protons does this element contain?

(b) How many neutrons will this element contain?

(c) Explain what will happen to the number of protons and neutrons in this element if it emits:

   (i) an alpha particle;

   (ii) a beta particle;

   (iii) gamma radiation.

3.79 (a) The following nuclear reaction takes place.

$$^{238}_{92}U \rightarrow {}^{234}_{90}Th$$

What type of radioactive particle was emitted in this decay?

(b) What type of radioactive particle was emitted in the following reaction?

$$^{210}_{82}Pb \rightarrow {}^{210}_{83}Bi$$

(c) (i) Where does the beta particle come from in a nuclear reaction?

   (ii) Why does the emission of gamma radiation not cause any change to the atomic or mass numbers of an element?

3.80 A nuclear reaction can consist of a decay chain where several radioactive particles are emitted as the radionuclides decay. Find the total number of alpha and beta particles emitted in the following decay series.

	Initial Element		Final Element
(a)	$^{238}_{92}U$	→	$^{234}_{91}Pa$
(b)	$^{238}_{92}U$	→	$^{234}_{92}U$
(c)	$^{226}_{88}Ra$	→	$^{214}_{82}Pb$
(d)	$^{218}_{84}Po$	→	$^{210}_{82}Pb$

3.81 A radioactive decay series begins with Thorium $^{234}_{90}Th$. After emitting 2 alpha particles and 2 beta particles it becomes Radium (Ra). What will be the atomic and mass numbers of the radium atom?

3.82 Complete the following table by filling in the missing values.

	Activity	Number of decays	Time
(a)		6×10^7	30 s
(b)	2 MBq	2.4×10^8	
(c)		4×10^7	30 minutes
(d)	500 kBq		2 hours

3.83 A radioactive substance has an activity of 12 kBq.

(a) How many decays will occur in 1 minute?

(b) The half-life of the substance is 3 days. How long will it take for the activity to drop to 375 Bq?

© P&N Publications

Fission and fusion

3.84 The equation for a nuclear reaction is given below.

$$^{235}_{92}U + ^{1}_{0}n \rightarrow ^{140}_{58}Ce + ^{94}_{40}Zr + ^{1}_{0}n + ^{1}_{0}n + \text{energy}$$

(a) State whether this is a fission or fusion reaction giving reasons for your answer.

(b) Explain the difference between a spontaneous fission reaction and an induced fission reaction.

(c) (i) Explain, using $E = mc^2$, how this nuclear reaction results in the production of energy.

  (ii) Using the information given below, and any other data required from Appendix (ii), calculate the energy released in the above nuclear reaction.

$$\begin{aligned}
\text{mass of } ^{235}_{92}U &= 390 \cdot 173 \times 10^{-27} \text{ kg} \\
\text{mass of } ^{140}_{58}Ce &= 232 \cdot 242 \times 10^{-27} \text{ kg} \\
\text{mass of } ^{94}_{40}Zr &= 155 \cdot 883 \times 10^{-27} \text{ kg} \\
\text{mass of } ^{1}_{0}n &= 1 \cdot 675 \times 10^{-27} \text{ kg}
\end{aligned}$$

3.85 The following reaction takes place in a nuclear reactor:

$$^{235}_{92}U + ^{1}_{0}n \rightarrow ^{131}_{54}Xe + ^{103}_{45}Rh + ^{1}_{0}n + ^{1}_{0}n + \text{energy}.$$

(a) Given the following masses, calculate the energy produced by a single reaction.

$$\begin{aligned}
\text{mass of } ^{235}_{92}U &= 390 \cdot 173 \times 10^{-27} \text{ kg} \\
\text{mass of } ^{131}_{54}Xe &= 217 \cdot 302 \times 10^{-27} \text{ kg} \\
\text{mass of } ^{103}_{45}Rh &= 170 \cdot 822 \times 10^{-27} \text{ kg} \\
\text{mass of } ^{1}_{0}n &= 1 \cdot 675 \times 10^{-27} \text{ kg}
\end{aligned}$$

(b) How many reactions would have to take place per second to produce a heat output of 50 MW?

3.86 The following reaction occurs in the Sun to produce energy:

$$^{2}_{1}H + ^{1}_{1}H \rightarrow ^{3}_{2}He.$$

(a) What type of nuclear reaction is this?

(b) Calculate the amount of energy produced as a result of this reaction using the data given below.

$$\begin{aligned}
\text{mass of } ^{2}_{1}H &= 3 \cdot 34 \times 10^{-27} \text{ kg} \\
\text{mass of } ^{1}_{1}H &= 1 \cdot 67 \times 10^{-27} \text{ kg} \\
\text{mass of } ^{3}_{2}He &= 5 \cdot 007 \times 10^{-27} \text{ kg}
\end{aligned}$$

© P&N Publications

Dosimetry and Safety

Absorbed dose, dose equivalent and effective dose equivalent

3.87 Complete the following table by filling in the missing values.

	Absorbed dose	Mass	Energy
(a)		4×10^{-2} kg	5×10^{-6} J
(b)	50×10^{-6} J kg^{-1}		0·1 mJ
(c)	5×10^{-6} Gy	30 g	
(d)	10 μGy	0·5 kg	

3.88 A tumour has a mass of 20 g and absorbs 0·6 J of energy during radiotherapy treatment. What was the absorbed dose?

3.89 A patient in a hospital is given a chest X-ray and receives a dose of 30 μGy.

(a) The mass of tissue absorbing the X-rays is 15 kg. What energy is absorbed by the patient from the X-rays?

(b) Hospitals are keen to reduce the amount of radiation absorbed by patients to as low a dose as possible. State **three** factors which affect the risk of biological harm from radiation.

3.90 The following table gives the quality factor for certain types of radiation.

Type of radiation	Quality factor, Q
X-rays	1
gamma rays	1
beta particles	1
slow neutrons	5
fast neutrons	10
alpha particles	20

(a) Why is it necessary to assign a quality factor to different types of radiation?

(b) Find the absorbed dose equivalent for the following radiation exposures.

	Absorbed dose	Type of radiation
(i)	10 μGy	alpha particles
(ii)	3 mGy	X-rays
(iii)	5×10^{-6} Gy	fast neutrons
(iv)	40 mGy	beta particles

© P&N Publications

3.91 A football player breaks his toe and has it placed in plaster. Over the six weeks it takes for the fracture to heal he receives three X-rays with each producing an absorbed dose of 50 μGy. What is the total dose equivalent he received during his treatment?

3.92 A welder uses radioactive materials to help detect welding faults in a pipeline. Over a period of a year he receives 6 mGy of gamma radiation and 0·5 mGy of alpha radiation. What is the total dose equivalent he receives for the year?

3.93 (*a*) A radiation worker with a mass of 50 kg absorbs 200 μJ of alpha radiation. What dose equivalent did she receive?

(*b*) During the course of her work she is allowed to receive a dose equivalent of 50 mSv per year to her abdomen but 750 mSv per year to her hands or feet. Why is there a difference in these maximum permitted doses?

3.94 What is the dose equivalent rate in Sv h^{-1} if a person is exposed to 40 Sv over a 5 day treatment period during treatment for a tumour?

3.95 A research worker receives a total of 8 μGy of alpha radiation during an experiment which lasts for 4 hours.

(*a*) What dose equivalent would be logged for his exposure during the experiment?

(*b*) What is the dose equivalent rate for this experiment?

3.96 A laboratory technician works with radioactive substances and receives a dose equivalent rate of 36 μSv h^{-1}. She is exposed to radiation for 4 hours per day and works 5 days each week for 46 weeks.

(*a*) (i) What will be the total dose equivalent she absorbs?

(ii) Why is the sievert a better unit for measuring exposure to radiation than the gray?

(*b*) The total dose of radiation the technician receives is made up of radiation from the substances she is working with and background radiation.

(i) Describe some of the sources of background radiation.

(ii) What is the annual dosage a person in Britain receives due to natural sources?

(iii) As a condition of her employment the technician must wear a badge which measures the dosage of radiation she receives. Why is this necessary?

Gamma ray absorption

3.97 An experiment is set up to find the effect of distance on the count rate from a radioactive source emitting gamma radiation. The apparatus used is shown below along with a table of results obtained.

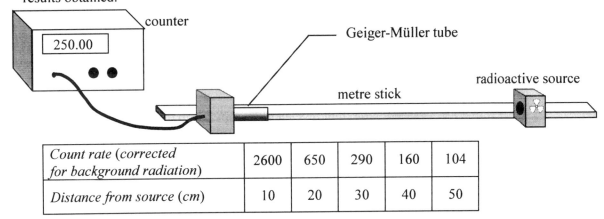

Count rate (corrected for background radiation)	2600	650	290	160	104
Distance from source (cm)	10	20	30	40	50

(a) Use these results to show that the count rate is inversely proportional to the square of the distance from the source.

(b) In carrying out this experiment a radioactive source was chosen which had a long half-life. Why was this necessary for the accuracy of the experiment?

(c) (i) Why must the readings be corrected for background radiation?

(ii) Name **two** sources of background radiation which may have affected this experiment.

3.98 An experiment is devised to demonstrate the effect of placing different thicknesses of metal in front of a radioactive source which emits only gamma radiation.

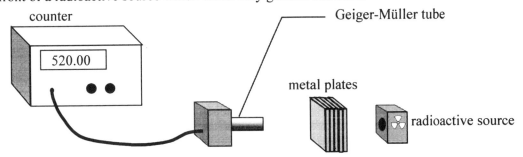

The distance between the radioactive source and the Geiger-Müller tube is constant throughout the experiment and the count rate is measured when different thicknesses of metal are placed between the detector and source. The background count is established with no source present.

The results obtained from the experiment are shown below.

Thickness of metal in cm	Count rate corrected for background count in counts per minute
0	800
0·5	520
1·0	340
1·5	220
2·0	140
2·5	86

© P&N Publications

3.98 (cont.)

(a) (i) Draw a graph of these results and hence find a value for the half-thickness of the metal for this source.

(ii) On the same axes, sketch the graph which might have been obtained if the count rate had not been corrected for background radiation.

(b) What effect would have been observed on the count rate if the distance between the source and the Geiger-Müller tube had been increased?

(c) The source used in this experiment has a very long half-life. Why would inaccurate results be obtained if a source with a very short half-life had been used?

3.99 An X–ray beam produces an dose equivalent of 500 μSv when used unshielded.

What would be the absorbed dose if a 6 mm thick copper screen was used in front of it which has a half-value thickness of 1 mm?

3.100 A composite material is used to shield a radioactive source. What is its half-value thickness if it reduces the activity of the source from 2 MBq to 125 kBq when the source is surrounded by shielding 16 cm thick?

3.101 A technician producing radioactive isotopes for medical use has to pick up a radioactive source and transfer it to a container. This is accomplished using a pair of tongs. A lead shield 12 mm thick is also available and can be placed between the technician and the source but increases the time it takes to carry out the transfer. The distance of the technician from the source is the same for both operations.

The dose equivalent rate for an unshielded source is 2 μSv s^{-1}. The transfer of the source will take 32 s to achieve if lead shielding is used but only 8 s if no shielding is used.

(a) Calculate the dose equivalent received by the technician when handling the source without the shielding.

(b) The half-thickness of lead for the source being handled is 4 mm. Calculate the dose equivalent when shielding is used.

(c) A second pair of tongs is available which allows the technician to double the distance between himself and the source but unfortunately does not permit the use of the lead shielding. Compare the dosage the technician would receive by using these tongs with the shorter, shielded tongs used in part (b) and hence make a recommendation on which he should use.

Uncertainties

1. A pupil sets out to measure the resistance of an electronic component using an ammeter and voltmeter. He uses a digital voltmeter to measure the voltage and a moving coil meter to measure the current.

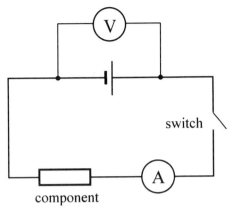

In making the measurements he makes the following mistakes:

   A. the ammeter is wrongly calibrated and reads a value 5% higher than the true value;
   B. the voltmeter has a loose connection and the reading varies as a result;
   C. the ammeter has several scales and the pupil reads the wrong scale for some of the readings.

   (a) State whether each of these uncertainties is a reading, systematic or random uncertainty.

   (b) To get a better value for the resistance of the component all the members of the class repeat his measurements. Why will this give a more accurate answer?

   (c) The following values are obtained for the voltage and current across the component.

Voltage (V)	Current (A)
8·9	0·52
8·9	0·51
9·0	0·52
8·9	0·53
8·7	0·51
8·8	0·52
8·9	0·54
8·8	0·52

   (i) Find:
   A the mean voltage;
   B the mean current.
   (ii) Hence find the best estimate of the resistance of the component.

   (d) What effect has a systematic uncertainty on the mean value obtained in the measurements?

2. All measuring instruments are subject to reading uncertainties. What is the reading uncertainty in the following instruments?

(a)

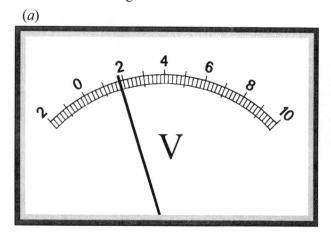

(b)

3. A pupil carries out an experiment to measure the charge stored on a capacitor at a certain voltage. She sets up the apparatus shown below.

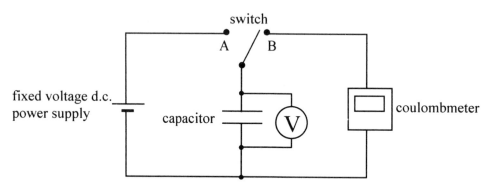

The capacitor is charged from a fixed voltage supply and then discharged into the coulomb meter to measure the charge it had stored. The following values for charge stored were obtained when a voltage of 1·5 V was used:

147 µC, 150 µC, 148 µC, 149 µC, 150 µC, 152 µC.

(a) Calculate the mean value from these measurements.

(b) Calculate the approximate random uncertainty in the mean value. Express the random uncertainty in the form of:

(i) an absolute uncertainty;

(ii) a percentage uncertainty.

4. An experiment is carried out to measure the specific heat capacity of water. The following mean values are obtained after repeating the experiment several times.

   Mass of water heated = 200 g ± 1 g.

   Temperature rise of water = 10°C ± 0·5°C.

   Energy added = 8600 J ± 100 J.

   (a) (i) Calculate the percentage uncertainty in each of the measurements above.

   (ii) Which quantity has the largest percentage uncertainty?

   (b) Calculate the value of specific heat capacity from these results. Give the final answer in the form of the value and:

   (i) the percentage uncertainty;

   (ii) the absolute uncertainty.

5. A pupil sets out to measure the wavelength of light by the use of a diffraction grating. The layout of her apparatus is shown below.

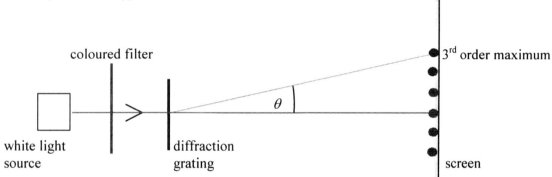

She obtains the following results:

angle θ = 18° ± 0·5 °

slit separation = 5×10^{-6} m ± 5×10^{-8} m.

(a) What is the percentage uncertainty in:

(i) the angle θ;

(ii) the slit separation?

(b) Using your answers to part (a), calculate the best estimate for the wavelength of the light. Include the **absolute** uncertainty in the final answer.

Appendix (i)—Higher Formulae

UNIT 1 Mechanics and Properties of Matter

Equations of Motion

$\bar{v} = \dfrac{s}{t}$ and $\bar{v} = \dfrac{u+v}{2}$ Average speed, u and v in m s^{-1}.

For uniformly accelerated motion,
$v = u + at$

$v^2 = u^2 + 2as$ v and u in m s^{-1}, a in m s^{-2}, s in m and t in s.

$s = ut + \tfrac{1}{2}at^2$

For a velocity v at an angle θ to the horizontal,
$v_h = v\cos\theta$ and $v_v = v\sin\theta$

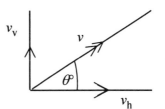

Newton's Second Law
$F_{un} = ma$ Force in N, mass in kg and acceleration in m s^{-2}

For an object of weight W on a slope inclined at angle θ to the horizontal,
$F_{perpendicular} = W\cos\theta$
$F_{parallel} = W\sin\theta$ Force in N.

Momentum and Impulse
momentum $= m \times v$ Momentum is in kg m s^{-1}, mass in kg and velocity in m s^{-1}.

impulse $= \bar{F} \times t$ Impulse in N s, average force in N and time in s.

impulse $= \Delta(mv)$ The unit for impulse can also be kg m s^{-1}.

Density and Pressure
$\rho = \dfrac{m}{V}$ Density is in kg m^{-3}, mass in kg and volume in m^3.

For pressure in a liquid, pressure $\propto$ density ($p \propto \rho$) and pressure $\propto$ depth ($p \propto h$)
so $p = \rho g h$

The Gas Laws
$p = \dfrac{F}{A}$ Pressure is in Pa, force in N and area in m^2.

$p_1 V_1 = p_2 V_2$ for a fixed mass of gas at constant temperature.

$\dfrac{p_1}{T_1} = \dfrac{p_2}{T_2}$ for a fixed mass of gas at constant volume and where temperature is in kelvin.

$\dfrac{V_1}{T_1} = \dfrac{V_2}{T_2}$ for a fixed mass of gas at constant pressure and where temperature is in kelvin.

$\dfrac{p_1 V_1}{T_1} = \dfrac{p_2 V_2}{T_2}$ for a fixed mass of gas where temperature is in kelvin.

© P&N Publications

UNIT 2 Electricity and Electronics
Electric Fields and Resistors in Circuits

$W = QV$ Work done (energy) in J, charge in C and voltage in V.

Resistors in a series circuit,
$R_{total} = R_1 + R_2 + R_3$ All resistance values in Ω or all in kΩ.

Resistance in a parallel circuit,
$\dfrac{1}{R_{total}} = \dfrac{1}{R_1} + \dfrac{1}{R_2} + \dfrac{1}{R_3}$ All resistance values in Ω or all in kΩ.

For a circuit with internal resistance,
$E = Ir + IR$ Current in A, resistance in Ω and E in V.

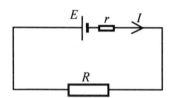

For a balanced Wheatstone bridge,
$\dfrac{P}{Q} = \dfrac{R}{S}$

For an out of balance Wheatstone bridge.
$\Delta R \propto V$

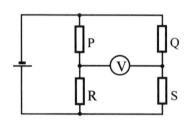

Alternating Current and Voltage

$V_{peak} = V_{rms} \times \sqrt{2}$ $\sqrt{2} \cong 1\cdot 4$

$V_{rms} = \dfrac{V_{peak}}{\sqrt{2}}$

The above formulae also apply to current.

Capacitance

$C = \dfrac{Q}{V}$ Capacitance in farads, charge in coulombs and voltage in volts.

$E = \tfrac{1}{2}QV = \tfrac{1}{2}CV^2 = \tfrac{1}{2}\dfrac{Q^2}{C}$ Energy in joules, capacitance in farads, charge in coulombs and voltage in volts.

$I \propto f$ for a capacitor   Current is independent of frequency for a resistor.

© P&N Publications

Analogue Electronics

Inverting Mode

$$\text{gain} = \frac{V_{out}}{V_1} = -\frac{R_f}{R_1}$$

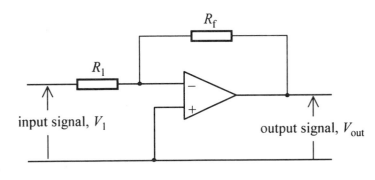

Differential Mode

$$V_{out} = (V_2 - V_1)\frac{R_f}{R_1}$$

provided $\quad \dfrac{R_f}{R_1} = \dfrac{R_3}{R_2}$

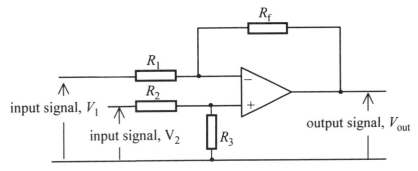

UNIT 3 Radiation and Matter

Waves

$f = \dfrac{1}{T}$ Frequency in Hz and time period in s.

For constructive interference
path difference = $n\lambda$ where $n = 0, 1, 2, 3, 4, 5, 6$ etc.

For destructive interference
path difference = $(n + \tfrac{1}{2})\lambda$ where $n = 0, 1, 2, 3, 4, 5, 6$ etc.

For the nth order fringe of a diffraction grating,
$n\lambda = d \sin \theta$ Wavelength and spacing in m.

Refraction of Light

When refraction occurs, the refractive index n is given by,

$$n = \frac{\sin \theta_1}{\sin \theta_2} = \frac{v_1}{v_2} = \frac{\lambda_1}{\lambda_2}$$

When total internal reflection occurs, the critical angle C is given by,

$$\sin C = \frac{1}{n}$$

© P&N Publications

Optoelectronics and Semiconductors

$I = \dfrac{P}{A}$ Intensity in W m^{-2}, power in W and area in m^2.

$I \propto \dfrac{1}{d^2}$
(i.e. $I_1 d_1^2 = I_2 d_2^2$) Intensity in W m^{-2} and d in m^2.

$E = hf$ Energy in J, h is Planck's constant = $6\cdot63 \times 10^{-34}$ J s, and frequency in hertz.

$I = Nhf$ Intensity in W m^{-2}, N is number of photons per second per unit area and f in Hz.

Work Function $= hf_o$ h is Planck's constant and f_o is the threshold frequency in Hz.

$E_k = hf - hf_o$ Kinetic energy in J, and f_o and f in Hz.

$E = W_2 - W_1 = hf$ Energy in J, W_1 and W_2 energy levels of electron in J, and frequency in Hz.

Nuclear Reactions

$^{\text{mass number } A}_{\text{atomic number } Z} Q$ A is number of neutrons + protons, Z is number of protons and Q is the chemical name.

Dosimetry and Safety

$A = \dfrac{N}{t}$ A is activity in becquerels (Bq).

$D = \dfrac{E}{m}$ D is the absorbed dose in grays (Gy).

$H = DQ$ H is the absorbed dose equivalent in sieverts (Sv).

$\dot{H} = \dfrac{H}{t}$ $\dot{H}$ is the absorbed dose equivalent rate in sieverts per hour (Sv h^{-1}).

$E = mc^2$ Where m is the mass defect and c is 3×10^8 m s^{-1}.

© P&N Publications

FORMULAE TO REMEMBER FROM STANDARD GRADE

wave speed = frequency × wavelength $\quad v = f\lambda$

speed = $\dfrac{\text{distance}}{\text{time}}$ $\quad v = \dfrac{d}{t}$

acceleration = $\dfrac{\text{change in speed}}{\text{time taken for change}}$

acceleration = $\dfrac{\text{final speed - initial speed}}{\text{time taken for change}}$ $\quad a = \dfrac{v-u}{t}$

weight = mass × gravitational field strength $\quad W = mg$

force = mass × acceleration $\quad F = ma$

work done = force × distance $\quad \text{work} = Fd$

power = $\dfrac{\text{energy transferred}}{\text{time}}$ $\quad P = \dfrac{E}{t}$

potential energy = mass × gravitational field strength × height $\quad E_p = mgh$

kinetic energy = ½ mass × velocity² $\quad E_k = \tfrac{1}{2}mv^2$

charge = current × time $\quad Q = It$

electrical energy = current × time × voltage $\quad E = ItV$

voltage = current × resistance $\quad V = IR \quad$ Ohm's Law

power = current × voltage $\quad P = IV$

power = current² × resistance $\quad P = I^2R$

power = $\dfrac{\text{voltage}^2}{\text{resistance}}$ $\quad$ power = $\dfrac{V^2}{R}$

electrical energy = power × time $\quad E = Pt$

total resistance (series) $\quad R_{total} = R_1 + R_2 + R_3$

total resistance (parallel) $\quad \dfrac{1}{R_{total}} = \dfrac{1}{R_1} + \dfrac{1}{R_2} + \dfrac{1}{R_3}$

voltage gain = $\dfrac{\text{voltage out}}{\text{voltage in}}$ $\quad$ voltage gain = $\dfrac{V_{out}}{V_{in}}$

power gain = $\dfrac{\text{power out}}{\text{power in}}$ $\quad$ power gain = $\dfrac{P_{out}}{P_{in}}$

© P&N Publications

% efficiency = $\dfrac{\text{energy out}}{\text{energy in}} \times 100$

Note: the formulae below, although in the Standard Grade course, are not covered by any of the content at Higher and so are only included for completeness.

$\dfrac{\text{turns in primary}}{\text{turns in secondary}} = \dfrac{\text{voltage in primary}}{\text{voltage in secondary}} \qquad \dfrac{n_p}{n_s} = \dfrac{V_p}{V_s}$

primary voltage × primary current = secondary voltage × secondary current $\qquad V_p \times I_p = V_s \times I_s$

$\dfrac{\text{turns in primary}}{\text{turns in secondary}} = \dfrac{\text{current in secondary}}{\text{current in primary}} \qquad \dfrac{n_p}{n_s} = \dfrac{I_s}{I_p}$

heat energy = specific heat capacity × mass × change in temperature $\qquad E_h = c\,m\,\Delta T$

heat energy = mass × specific latent heat $\qquad E_h = m\,l$

© P&N Publications

Appendix (ii)—Units and Abbreviations

When answering questions ensure that the correct SI unit is used after every numerical answer e.g. velocity is measured in m s^{-1} and acceleration in m s^{-2} etc.
All the ones that you will use in this course are given in the table below.

Quantity	SI Unit	Abbreviation
Velocity	metres per second	m s^{-1}
Speed	metres per second	m s^{-1}
Distance	metres	m
Displacement	metres	m
Time	seconds	s
Acceleration	metres per second per second	m s^{-2}
Force	newtons	N
Momentum	kilograms metres per second	kg m s^{-1}
Impulse	newton seconds, kilograms metres per second	N s, kg m s^{-1}
Mass	kilograms	kg
Pressure	pascals, newtons per square metre	Pa, N m^{-2}
Area	square metres	m^2
Volume	cubic metres	m^3
Temperature	kelvin, degrees celsius	K, °C
Density	kilograms per cubic metre	kg m^{-3}
Work, Energy	joules	J
Power	watts, joules per second	W, J s^{-1}
Charge	coulombs	C
Voltage or potential difference	volts	V
Current	amperes	A
Resistance	ohms	Ω
Capacitance	farads	F
Frequency	hertz	Hz
Period	seconds	s
Wavelength	metres	m
Intensity	watts per square metre	W m^{-2}
Activity	becquerels	Bq
Absorbed dose	grays	Gy
Absorbed dose equivalent	sieverts	Sv
Absorbed dose equivalent rate	sieverts per hour	Sv h^{-1}

Appendix (iii)—Data Sheet

COMMON PHYSICAL QUANTITIES

Quantity	Symbol	Value	Quantity	Symbol	Value
Speed of light in vacuum	c	3.00×10^8 m s^{-1}	Speed of sound in air	v	340 m s^{-1}
Magnitude of charge on electron	e	1.60×10^{-19} C	Mass of electron	m_e	9.11×10^{-31} kg
Gravitational acceleration	g	9.8 m s^{-2}	Mass of neutron	m_n	1.675×10^{-27} kg
Planck's constant	h	6.63×10^{-34} J s	Mass of proton	m_p	1.673×10^{-27} kg

REFRACTIVE INDICES

The refractive indices refer to sodium light of wavelength 589 nm and to substances at a temperature of 273 K.

Substance	Refractive index	Substance	Refractive index
Diamond	2.42	Glycerol	1.47
Glass	1.51	Water	1.33
Ice	1.31	Air	1.00
Perspex	1.49		

SPECTRAL LINES

Element	Wavelength/nm	Colour	Element	Wavelength/nm	Colour
Hydrogen	656	Red	Cadmium	644	Red
	486	Blue–green		509	Green
	434	Blue–violet		480	Blue
	410	Violet		Lasers	
	397	Ultraviolet	Element	Wavelength/nm	Colour
	389	Ultraviolet	Carbon dioxide	9550	Infrared
				10590	Infrared
Sodium	589	Yellow	Helium–neon	633	Red

PROPERTIES OF SELECTED MATERIALS

Substance	Density/ kg m^{-3}	Melting Point/ K	Boiling Point/ K	Specific Heat Capacity/ J kg^{-1} K^{-1}	Specific Latent Heat of Fusion/ J kg^{-1}	Specific Latent Heat of Vaporisation/ J kg^{-1}
Aluminium	2.70×10^3	933	2623	9.02×10^2	3.95×10^5	....
Copper	8.96×10^3	1357	2853	3.86×10^2	2.05×10^5	....
Glass	2.60×10^3	1400	....	6.70×10^2	....	....
Ice	9.20×10^2	273	....	2.10×10^3	3.34×10^5	....
Glycerol	1.26×10^3	291	563	2.43×10^3	1.81×10^5	8.30×10^5
Methanol	7.91×10^2	175	338	2.52×10^3	9.9×10^4	1.12×10^6
Sea Water	1.02×10^3	264	377	3.93×10^3	....	....
Water	1.00×10^3	273	373	4.19×10^3	$3.34 \times\times 10^5$	2.26×10^6
Air	1.29	....	....	....	....	....
Hydrogen	9.0×10^{-2}	14	20	1.43×10^4	....	4.50×10^5
Nitrogen	1.25	63	77	1.04×10^3	....	2.00×10^5
Oxygen	1.43	55	90	9.18×10^2	....	2.40×10^5

The gas densities refer to a temperature of 273 K and a pressure of 1.01×10^5 Pa.

© P&N Publications

Appendix (iv)—Answers to Numerical Problems

UNIT 1 Mechanics and Properties of Matter

Vectors

1.1 Vector – (iii), (iv), (vii), (viii) and (ix).
Scalar – (i), (ii), (v), (vi), (x).

1.2 (a) (i) 140 m.
    (ii) $v = 7$ m s^{-1}.
(b) (i) 90 m.
    (ii) $v = 4.5$ m s^{-1} forwards.
(c) (i) 0 m.
    (ii) 0 m s^{-1}.

1.3 (a) 854 m at 020·6°.
(b) 045°.

1.4 (a) (i) 152 cm at 067°.
    (ii) 22·4 m at 063°.
    (iii) 16·3 m at 068°.
    (iv) 25·5 m at 079°.
(b) (i) 18 m s^{-1} at 056°.
    (ii) 37 m s^{-1} at 065°.
    (iii) 22 m s^{-1} at 102°.
    (iv) 14·7 m s^{-1} at 066°.

1.5 (a) (i) 10·4 m s^{-1}.
    (ii) 6 m s^{-1}.
(b) (i) 54·4 m.
    (ii) 25·4 m.

1.6 Resultant velocity of 5·8 ms^{-1} at 059°.
1.7 Resultant displacement of 2·75 m at 057°.
1.8 1·6 m s^{-1} at 218°.
1.9 (a) (i) 125·6 m s^{-1}.
    (ii) 33·6 m s^{-1}.
(b) (i) 300 km.
    (ii) 258 km at 028·5°.
    (iii) $v = 107·5$ m s^{-1} at 028°.
(c) 90·4 m s^{-1} at 034·5°.

1.10 (a) (i) $v_h = 1039$ m s^{-1}
    (ii) Horizontal component will increase.
(b) 20·9 m s^{-2} at 23·9° below the initial acceleration or 6·1° above the horizontal.

Equations of Motion

1.12 (b) Uniform acceleration.
(c) $a = -9·81$ m s^{-2}.
(d) (i) height = 4·9 m.
    (ii) height = 6·5 m.
    (iii) 1·6 m.

1.13 (a) C.
1.15 (a) $t = 20$ s.
(b) $v = 16$ m s^{-1}.
(c) $a = 2$ m s^{-2}.
(d) $u = 5$ m s^{-1}.

1.16 (a) $a = 2·5$ m s^{-2}.
(b) $s = 75\,000$ m.
(c) $v = 1·79$ m s^{-1}.
(d) $u = 20$ m s^{-1}.

1.17 (a) $s = 125$ m.
(b) $u = 40$ m s^{-1}.
(c) $t = 10·95$ s.
(d) $a = 245$ m s^{-2}.

1.18 $u = 8$ m s^{-1}.
1.19 $a = -0·4$ m s^{-2}.
1.20 $a = -4$ m s^{-2}.
1.21 $a = 2·78$ m s^{-2}.
1.22 $s = 187·1$ m.
1.23 $a = 8333$ m s^{-2}.
1.24 $s = -30·6$ m i.e. 30·6 m downwards.
1.25 $s = -0·82$ m.

1.26 (a) 0 m s^{-1}.
(b) $s = 10$ m.
(c) -14 m s^{-1}.
(d) $t = 2·86$ s.

1.27 (b) $s = -32·1$ m.
(c) $v = -25·4$ m s^{-1}.

1.28 (a) $t = 1·53$ s.
(b) $s = 11·5$ m.
(c) $s = 8·21$ m above the ground.

1.29 (a) $t = 12·2$ s.
(b) $s = 183·7$ m.

1.30 (a) (i) Constant velocity.
    (ii) Uniform acceleration.
(b) (i) 0 m s^{-1}.
    (ii) $v = 5·9$ m s^{-1}.
(c) $v_R = 100·2$ m s^{-1} $\theta = 3·4°$.

1.31 (a) $t = 0·64$ s.
(b) $s = 3·83$ m.
(c) $v_R = 8·68$ m s^{-1} $\theta = 46·3°$.

1.32 (a) $v = 7$ m s^{-1}.
(b) $t = 0·71$ s.
(c) $v = 16·9$ m s^{-1}.

1.33 (a) $v_v = 199·2$ m s^{-1}.
(b) $v_h = 115$ m s^{-1}.

1.34 (a) (i) $v_v = 12·5$ m s^{-1}.
    (ii) $v_h = 21·6$ m s^{-1}.
(b) (i) 0 m s^{-1}.
    (ii) 21·6 m s^{-1}.
(c) $s = 7·97$ m.
(d) (i) $t = 1·28$ s.
    (ii) 2·56 s.

1.35 (a) (i) $v_h = 13·1$ m s^{-1}.
    (ii) $v_v = 4·8$ m s^{-1}.
(b) $t = 0·49$ s.
(c) $t = 0·98$ s.
(d) $s = 12·86$ m.

1.36 (c) $a = -8·5$ m s^{-2}.
(d) Height = 0·17 m.
(e) Range = 1·44 m.
(f) $v_R = 4$ m s^{-1} $\theta = 25·3°$.

1.37 (a) (i) $v = 26·7$ m s^{-1}.
    (ii) $v_R = 29·5$ m s^{-1} at 25° above the horizontal.

© P&N Publications

1.38 (a) $s = -1.18$.
　　(b) $s = 0.7$ m.
1.39 (a) (i) $u = 12.25$ m s^{-1}.
　　　　(ii) $v_h = 8.66$ m s^{-1}.
　　(b) $s = 21.65$ m.

Newton's Second Law, Energy and Power

1.40 $a = 2.5$ m s^{-2}.
1.41 (a) $a = 5$ m s^{-2}.
　　(b) Puck continues at a constant velocity.
1.42 (a) $F = 30$ N.
　　(b) $F = 18$ N.
　　(c) Tension T_1 will now be 40 N.
1.43 (a) $W = 3136$ N.
　　(b) 3136 N.
　　(c) $a = 0.46$ m s^{-2}.
1.44 (b) $T = 2800$ N.
　　(c) 2744 N.
1.45 (b) (i) $F = 35$ N.
　　　　(ii) resultant = 40.3 N at an angle of 60° to wind force.
1.46 (a) $W = 14.7$ N.
　　(b) $a = 50.2$ m s^{-2}.
　　(c) (i) Increasing upwards acceleration.
　　　　(ii) Uniformly accelerating downwards.
1.47 (a) $W = 686$ N.
　　(b) (i) 721 N.
　　　　(ii) 686 N.
　　　　(iii) 616 N.
　　(c) (i) 12 360 N.
　　　　(ii) 11 760 N.
　　　　(iii) 10 560 N.
1.48 (a) 90 N acting downwards.
　　(b) accelerating downwards at 2 m s^{-2}.
1.49 (a) $a = 2.56$ m s^{-2} at 38.7° above the horizontal.
　　(b) $a = 256$ m s^{-2} at 51.3° above the horizontal.
　　(c) $a = 3.63$ m s^{-2} horizontally.
1.50 tension = 3000 N.
1.51 $a = 1.96$ m s^{-2}.
1.52 (a) $W = 19.6$ N
　　　　$W_{PARALLEL} = 9.8$ N
　　　　$W_{PERPENDICULAR} = 17$ N.
　　(b) $W = 98$ N
　　　　$W_{PARALLEL} = 33.5$ N
　　　　$W_{PERPENDICULAR} = 92$ N.
　　(c) $W = 2.45$ N
　　　　$W_{PARALLEL} = 1.23$ N
　　　　$W_{PERPENDICULAR} = 2.12$ N.
　　(d) $W = 9.8$ N
　　　　$W_{PARALLEL} = 6.93$ N
　　　　$W_{PERPENDICULAR} = 6.93$ N.
1.53 (a) $W_{PARALLEL} = 20.3$ N.
　　(b) 20.3 N.
1.54 Friction = 185.4 N.

1.55 (a) (i) $W_{PERPENDICULAR} = 7828$ N.
　　　　(ii) $W_{PARALLEL} = 2849$ N.
　　(b) $F = 382.5$ N.
　　(d) Friction = 2466.5 N.
1.56 (a) Tension$_{VERTICAL}$ = 6.3 N.
　　(b) Tension$_{HORIZONTAL}$ = 13.6 N.
1.57 (a) $W_{PARALLEL} = 9.8$ N.
　　(b) $W = 14.7$ N.
　　(c) Tension = 14.7 N.
　　(d) friction = 4.9 N.

Momentum and Impulse

1.58 Mom = 9 600 kg m s^{-1}.
1.59 $m = 60$ kg.
1.60 $v = 20$ m s^{-1}.
1.61 $v = 1.2$ m s^{-1}.
1.62 $v = 2.0$ m s^{-1}.
1.63 $u_A = 5.25$ m s^{-1}.
1.64 $m_B = 0.138$ kg.
1.65 $v_B = 5.25$ m s^{-1} to the right.
1.66 $v_B = 0.3$ m s^{-1} in the direction the first ball was travelling.
1.67 $v_1 = 0.3$ m s^{-1} to the left.
1.69 $v_1 = 96$ m s^{-1}.
1.72 (a) $v_A = -0.17$ m s^{-1} (0.17 m s^{-1} to the left.)
1.73 (a) Impulse = 4.0 N s.
　　　　Change in momentum = 4.0 kg m s^{-1}.
　　(b) $t = 5$ s.
　　　　Change in momentum = 30 kg m s^{-1}.
　　(c) $F = 0.5$ N.
　　(d) $F = 200$ N.
　　　　Change in momentum = 2 kg m s^{-1}.
1.74 Impulse = 6.0 N s.
1.75 $t = 0.8$ s.
1.76 (a) Impulse = 6 N s.
　　(b) (i) Change in momentum = 6 kg m s^{-1}.
　　　　(ii) $\Delta v = 20.7$ m s^{-1}.
1.78 (a) (i) Impulse = 1.5 kg m s^{-1}.
　　　　(ii) $F = 10.0$ N.
　　(b) $a = 2.0$ m s^{-2}.
　　(c) initial velocity of ball = 2.6 m s^{-1}.

Density and Pressure

1.79 (a) $\rho = 1.3$ kg m^{-3}.
　　(b) $m = 4.5 \times 10^{-4}$ kg.
　　(c) $V = 6.3 \times 10^{-2}$ m^3.
　　(d) $m = 0.36$ kg.
　　(e) $V = 8.8 \times 10^{-2}$ m^3.
1.80 3.6 kg.
1.81 0.92 kg litre^{-1}.
1.82.(a) $m = 0.1$ kg.
　　(c) $\rho = 947$ kg m^{-3}.
1.84 (a) (ii) $\rho = 1.25$ kg m^{-3}.
　　(c) (i) 1000 cm^3

1.85 (a) $p = 2000$ Pa.
(b) $p = 15\,000$ Pa.
(c) $F = 10$ N.
(d) $F = 3$ N.
(e) area = 0.0625 m^2.
1.86 $p = 980$ Pa.
1.87 (a) Area in m^2 = 0.1×10^{-6} m^2.
(b) $p = 1.5 \times 10^8$ Pa.
1.88 (a) $100\,000$ Nm^{-2}.
(b) $F = 1500$ N.
1.89 Approximately, $p = 500\,000$ Pa.
1.93 (a) Mass which can be lifted is 315 kg.
1.94 236 N.

The Gas Laws

1.95 (a) $V_2 = 0.125$ m^3.
(b) $p_2 = 25 \times 10^5$ Pa.
(c) $V_1 = 16.67$ cm^3.
(d) $p_1 = 5 \times 10^5$ Pa.
(e) $p_2 = 1$ kPa.
1.96 $V_2 = 0.035$ m^3.
1.99 $p_2 = 4 \times 10^6$ Pa.
1.101 $-273°$C
1.102 (a) $p_2 = 3 \times 10^5$ Pa.
(b) $T_2 = 600$ K.
(c) $T_1 = 267$ K.
(d) $p_1 = 26.8$ kPa.
(e) $p_2 = 0$ Pa.
1.103 $p_2 = 8.3 \times 10^5$ Pa.
1.104 (b) $T_2 = 1450$ K.
1.105 (a) $p_2 = 467$ kPa.
1.106 (a) $V_2 = 4000$ cm^3.
1.107 293 K
1.108 (a) $V_2 = 2$ m^3.
(b) $T_1 = 1200$ K.
(c) $V_2 = 5.3$ litres.
(d) $V_1 = 2.5$ m^3.
(e) $T_2 = 2048$ K.
1.109 $V_2 = 5.25$ litres.
1.110 $V_2 = 5.4$ litres.
1.111 (b) (i) A $-273°$C
B 0 K
1.112 (d) $T_1 = 265$ K.
1.114 (a) $V_2 = 0.3$ m^3.
(b) $p_2 = 5 \times 10^6$ Pa.
(c) $T_2 = 24$ K.
(d) $V_2 = 2.7$ litres.
(e) $p_1 = 6.25 \times 10^6$ Pa.
(f) $T_1 = 15.3$ K ($-257.7°$C).
1.115 $V_2 = 12$ litres.
1.116 $V_2 = 6.2 \times 10^{-7}$ m^3.
1.117 $T_2 = 230.6$ K ($-42.4°$C).
1.118 New pressure is 8×10^5 Pa.

© P&N Publications

UNIT 2 Electricity and Electronics
Electric fields and resistors in circuits

2.2 (a) $W = 0.5$ J.
(b) $W = 0.2$ J.
(c) $V = 5 \times 10^{-5}$ V.
(d) $Q = 1 \times 10^{-3}$ C.
2.3 (a) (i) $Q = 1 \times 10^{-5}$ C.
(ii) 6.25×10^{13} electrons.
(b) $W = 5 \times 10^{-3}$ J.
2.4 (a) $W = 3.52 \times 10^{-15}$ J.
(b) $v = 8.8 \times 10^7$ ms^{-1}.
2.5 (a) $W = 3.2 \times 10^{-16}$ J.
(b) 3.2×10^{-16} J.
(c) $v = 2.65 \times 10^7$ ms^{-1}.
2.8 (a) $E = 11$ V.
(b) $r = 5$ Ω.
(c) $R = 29.3$ Ω.
(d) $I = 0.5$ A.
2.9 $I = 0.2$ A.
2.10 (a) $I = 0.5$ A.
(b) t.p.d. = 5 V.
(c) lost volts = 1 V.
2.11 (a) $I = 0.27$ A.
(b) (i) $P = 0.37$ W.
(ii) $P = 0.04$ W.
2.12 (c) $r = 0.93$ Ω.
2.13 (a) (i) Emf = 0.46 V.
(ii) internal resistance = 8 Ω.
(b) (ii) $I = 57.5$ mA.
2.14 (b) $r = 2$ Ω.
2.15 (a) 1.45 V—when no current is being drawn.
(b) $r = 0.3$ Ω.
(c) (i) Increases.
(ii) Increases.
(iii) Decreases
2.16 (a) (i) $Q = 216\,000$ C.
(ii) $E = 2.6$ MJ.
(b) (i) $r = 0.0375$ Ω.
(ii) 6.25×10^{-3} Ω.
(iii) $P = 240$ W.
(c) (i) A. 2.1 Ω.
B. 0.4 Ω.
2.19 (a) 40 Ω.
(b) 4 kΩ.
(c) 45 Ω.
2.20 (a) $I = 0.05$ A.
(b) $V_1 = 0.5$ V.
$V_2 = 1.0$ V.
(c) (i) $I = 0.033$ A.
(ii) $I = 0.017$ A.
(d) $P = 0.075$ W.
2.21 (a) (i) Between A and D to give 9 V.
(ii) Between B and C $V = 2$V.
(b) $P = 0.06$ W.
2.22 $R_{TOTAL} = 3.3 \times 10^{-6}$ Ω.

2.23 (a) Total resistance of circuit is 3000 Ω.
  (i) $V = 4$ V.
  (ii) $V = 8$ V.
 (b) (i) $V = 8.57$ V.
  (ii) $V = 3.43$ V.
2.24 (a) Decrease.
 (b) 30 Ω.
2.25 $R_1 = 10$ Ω.
 $R_2 = 10$ Ω.
 $R_3 = 2$ Ω.
 $R_4 = 2$ Ω.
2.26 (a) $R = 15$ Ω.
 (b) Potentiometer.
 (c) (i) $P = 0.26$ W.
  (ii) $P = 0.15$ W.
2.27 (a) 3·5 V.
 (b) $R_2 = 50$ Ω.
 (c) (ii) $V = 1.16$ V.
2.28 (a) $R_1/R_2 = R_3/R_4$.
 (b) 0 V.
2.29 (a) $Rx = 125$ Ω.
 (b) $Rx = 750$ Ω.
 (c) $Rx = 840$ Ω.
 (d) $Rx = 1500$ Ω.
2.30 (a) $R_3 = 24$ Ω.
 (b) (i) Yes.
  (ii) 4·5 V across bulb.
  (iii) $R_3 = 48$ Ω.
2.31 (a) $Rx = 1.2$ kΩ.
2.32 (b) (i) $R_3 = 480$ Ω.
  (iii) A. No effect.
   B. No effect.
   C. Increases sensitivity.
2.33 $Rx = 245$ Ω.
2.34 (a) $R_V = 305$ Ω.
 (c) Change in resistance required = 15 Ω.

Alternating current and voltage

2.36 (a) $f = 50$ Hz.
 (b) $f = 250$ Hz.
2.37 $V_{peak} = 336$ V.
2.38 $I_{rms} = 0.2$ A.
2.39 $V_{peak} = 8.4$ V.
 $I_{peak} = 0.28$ A.
2.40 (a) $I_{peak} = 0.125$ A.
 (b) $I_{rms} = 89 \times 10^{-3}$ A.
 (c) Current amplitude will not change.
2.41 (a) $V_{peak} = 16.8$ V.
 (b) $I_{rms} = 0.2$ A.
 (c) (i) Power$_{rms}$ = 2·4 W.

Capacitance

2.42 (c) $C = 2.2 \times 10^{-6}$ F.
2.43 (a) $C = 2.0 \times 10^{-5}$ F.
 (b) $C = 5 \times 10^{-8}$ F.
 (c) $V = 24\,000$ V.
 (d) $Q = 0.08$ C.
2.44 $Q = 1.2 \times 10^{-10}$ C.
2.45 $C = 2.5 \times 10^{-3}$ F.
2.46 $V = 25\,000$ V.
2.47 (a) 6 V.
 (b) $I = 3 \times 10^{-4}$ A.
2.48 (a) $I = 0.15$ A.
 (b) (i) 0 V.
  (ii) 1·5 V.
 (c) (i) 1·5 V.
  (ii) 0 V.
2.49 (b) (i) $Q = 1.5 \times 10^{-3}$ C.
  (ii) $E = 1.13 \times 10^{-3}$ J.
 (c) (i) $I = 0.027$ A.
2.51 $E = 0.2$ J.
2.52 $E = 1.25 \times 10^{-2}$ J.
2.53 $E = 0.02$ J.
2.54 (a) $C = 22$ μF.
 (b) $V_{rms} = 11.4$ V.
2.55 (a) $Q = 1.2 \times 10^{-6}$ C.
 (b) $E = 7.2 \times 10^{-6}$ J.
 (c) $W = 1.44 \times 10^{-5}$ J.
2.56 (a) $V = 16$ V.
 (b) $Q = 8 \times 10^{-3}$ C.
2.57 (a) $V = 50$ V.
 (b) $E = 1.25 \times 10^{-2}$ J.
2.58 (a) $V = 346$ V.
 (b) $Q = 1.73 \times 10^{-2}$ C.
2.61 (a) (i) $I = 0.01$ A.
  (ii) $Q = 5 \times 10^{-4}$ C.
  (iii) $E = 1.25 \times 10^{-3}$ J.
2.65 (a) 6·0 V.
2.66 (a) $E = 50$ J.
 (b) $\Delta T = 131.6$ °C.
2.67 $t = 5500$ s.

Analogue Electronics

2.69 (c) $V_o = -0.5$ V.
2.70 (a) $V_o = -5$ V.
 (b) $V_o = -0.4$ V.
 (c) $V_1 = 0.04$ V.
 (d) $R_f = 100$ kΩ.
 (e) $R_1 = 500$ Ω.
 (f) $V_o = 10$ V.
2.71 (a) 0 V.
 (b) (i) $V_o = -0.025$ V.
  (ii) $R_f = 10 \times 10^6$ Ω. (10 MΩ).
2.72 (a) (i) gain = −30.
  (ii) $R_f = 300$ kΩ.
2.73 (a) (i) $V_o = -10$ V.
2.74 (a) over all gain = 1500.
 (b) $V_o = 3$ V.

2.75 (a) $V_o = -2$ V.
     (b) $V_o = 1$ V
2.77 (a) Differential mode.
     (b) (i) $V_o = 2$ V.
         (ii) $V_o = -2$ V.
2.78 (a) $V_o = 1$ V.
     (b) $V_o = 2$ V.
     (c) $V_o = -3$ V.
     (d) $V_o = -0.6$ V.
2.79 (a) $V_o = (V_2 - V_1) R_f/R_1$.
     (b) (i) $V_o = 1$ V.
         (ii) $V_o = -5$ V.
         (iii) output cannot exceed 15 V.
2.80 (a) $R_f = 50\,000\ \Omega$ (50 kΩ).
     (b) $V_o = -4$ V.
2.82 (a) $R_V = 1$ kΩ.
     (b) $(V_2 - V_1) = 0.018$ V.
2.83 (a) (i) Differential.
         (ii) $V_o = (V_2 - V_1) R_f/R_1$.
     (b) gain = 200.
2.84 (a) (i) $R_{THERMISTOR} = 62.5$ kΩ.
         (ii) 0 V.

Unit 3—Radiation and Matter

Waves
3.1 $T = 5 \times 10^{-4}$ s.
3.2 $f = 1.25$ Hz.
3.3 (a) $f = 1 \times 10^{10}$ Hz.
    (b) $T = 1 \times 10^{-10}$ s.
3.4 (a) 512 Hz.
3.6 (a) A Constructive interference
        B Constructive interference
        C Destructive interference.
3.9 (c) (ii) A. A maximum.
             B. A maximum.
             C. A minimum.
3.10 (a) $\lambda = 0.1$ m.
3.11 2.9 m.
3.13 (b) (i) $\lambda = 2.8$ cm.
         (ii) $f = 1.07 \times 10^{10}$ Hz.
3.15 (a) (i) $\lambda = 5.95 \times 10^{-7}$ m (595 nm).
         (ii) $\theta = 26.1°$.
         (iii) $d = 2.48 \times 10^{-6}$ m.
         (iv) $\theta = 8°$.
     (b) (ii) green (iii) violet (iv) red.
3.16 $\theta = 27.9°$.
3.17 Number of lines per mm = 252.
3.18 3rd order fringe was being looked at.
3.19 Interference.
3.20 (b) 400 nm.
     (c) $\theta = 17.6°$.
3.21 (a) $\lambda = 5.5 \times 10^{-7}$ m (550 nm).

3.22 (a) $n = 1.52$.
     (b) $n = 1.47$.
     (c) $n = 1.53$.
     (d) $n = 1.63$.
3.23 (a) $\theta_{glass} = 22.5°$.
     (b) $\theta_{air} = 32.0°$.
     (c) $\theta_{air} = 49.5°$.
     (d) $\theta_{air} = 24.5°$.
3.24 $n = 1.61$.
3.25 (b) $n = 1.55$.
3.26 $\theta_{glass} = 20.7°$.
3.27 $\lambda_{glass} = 267$ nm.
3.28 (a) 3×10^8 m s^{-1}.
     (b) $v_{glass} = 2.02 \times 10^8$ m s^{-1}.
     (c) Frequency remains at 6×10^{14} Hz.
3.29 (a) A. red.
         B. violet.
     (b) (i) Ray A. $n = 1.52$.
         (ii) Ray B. $n = 1.55$.
     (c) (i) Unchanged.
         (ii) Increases.
         (iii) Increases.
3.32 $n = 1.49$.
3.33 Critical angle = 48.7°.
3.35 (a) (i) $n = 1.51$.
         (ii) $n = 1.54$.
     (b) (i) critical angle = 41.5°.
         (ii) critical angle = 40.5°.

Optoelectronics and semiconductors
3.37 (a) $I = 1$ W m^{-2}.
     (b) $I = 12.5$ W m^{-2}.
     (c) area = 0.17 m^2.
     (d) $P = 0.048$ W.
     (e) area = 13.3 m^2.
3.38 $I = 50$ W m^{-2}.
3.39 Area = 0.2 m^2.
3.40 (a) $I_1 = 0.64$ W m^{-2}.
     (b) $I_2 = 2.5$ W m^{-2}.
     (c) $d_2 = 4$ m.
     (d) $d_1 = 0.18$ m.
     (e) $I_2 = 128$ W m^{-2}.
3.42 $I_2 = 0.05$ W m^{-2}.
3.43 $d_2 = 8$ m.
3.44 (c) $I_2 = 4$ V.
3.47 $E = 5.7 \times 10^{-19}$ J.
3.48 $f = 5 \times 10^{14}$ Hz.
3.49 (b) (i) $f = 1.2 \times 10^{15}$ Hz.
     (c) (i) $E = 3.5 \times 10^{-19}$ J.
         (ii) Kinetic energy.
3.50 $f = 6.8 \times 10^{14}$ Hz.
3.51 work function = 3.4×10^{-19} J.
3.52 (a) work function = 1.66×10^{-20} J.
3.53 (a) $E_k = 4.9 \times 10^{-21}$ J.
     (b) $v = 1.04 \times 10^5$ m s^{-1}.

© P&N Publications

3.54 $I = 3.98$ W m^{-2}.
3.55 (a) $E = 4.97 \times 10^{-19}$ J.
 (b) 2×10^{14} photons.
3.56 (a) $E = 7.8 \times 10^{-19}$ J.
 (b) 1.8×10^{10} photons.
3.58 (a) 6.
 (b) (i) $\lambda = 1.51 \times 10^{-7}$ m.
  (ii) $\lambda = 1.36 \times 10^{-6}$ m.
3.59 (b) $E = 3.38 \times 10^{-19}$ J.
  $E = 3.37 \times 10^{-19}$ J.
  Two values for photon energy are almost identical.
3.61 (c) $E = 3.34 \times 10^{-19}$ J.
3.63 (b) (i) $E = 3.03 \times 10^{-19}$ J.
  (ii) Red.
3.66 $\lambda = 9.47 \times 10^{-6}$ m.
3.67 (a) $E = 3.14 \times 10^{-19}$ J.
 (b) (i) 318.3 W m^{-2}.
  (ii) 3.2×10^{15} photons.
3.68 (a) (i) $E = 2.4 \times 10^{-16}$ J.
3.70 (a) Diode (or p–n junction).
 (b) (i) Reverse biased.
  (ii) No reading.
3.71 (b) (i) $E = 3.04 \times 10^{-19}$ J.
  (ii) Heat energy.
  (iii) $\lambda = 5.0 \times 10^{-7}$ m. green light.
3.73 (b) $I_2 = 1.56 \times 10^{-6}$ A.
3.75 (a) $V_{gate} = 4$ V.

Nuclear Reactions

3.78 (a) 92.
 (b) 146.
3.79 (a) An alpha particle.
 (b) A beta particle.
3.80 (a) 1 alpha, 1 beta.
 (b) 1 alpha, 2 beta.
 (c) 3 alpha.
 (d) 2 alpha, 2 beta.
3.81 $^{226}_{88}$Ra .
3.82 (a) $A = 2 \times 10^6$ Bq.
 (b) $t = 120$ s.
 (c) 2.2×10^4 Bq.
 (d) $N = 3.6 \times 10^9$.
3.83 (a) $N = 720\,000$.
 (b) total time taken = 15 days.
3.84 (a) Fission.
 (c) (ii) 3.36×10^{-11} J.
3.85 (a) 3.37×10^{-11} J.
 (b) 1.49×10^{18} reactions per second.
3.86 (a) Fusion reaction.
 (b) 2.7×10^{-13} J.

Dosimetry and Safety

3.87 (a) $D = 1.25 \times 10^{-4}$ Gy.
 (b) $m = 2$ kg.
 (c) $E = 1.5 \times 10^{-7}$ J.
 (d) $E = 5.0 \times 10^{-6}$ J.
3.88 $D = 30$ Gy.
3.89 (a) $E = 4.5 \times 10^{-4}$ J.
3.90 (b) (i) $H = 2 \times 10^{-4}$ Sv.
  (ii) $H = 3 \times 10^{-3}$ Sv.
  (iii) $H = 5 \times 10^{-5}$ Sv.
  (iv) $H = 4 \times 10^{-2}$ Sv.
3.91 1.5×10^{-4} Sv.
3.92 16×10^{-3} Sv.
3.93 (a) $H = 80$ μSv.
3.94 $\dot{H} = 0.33$ Sv h^{-1}.
3.95 (a) $H = 1.6 \times 10^{-4}$ Sv.
 (b) $\dot{H} = 4 \times 10^{-5}$ Sv h^{-1}.
3.96 (a) (i) 3.3×10^{-2} Sv.
 (b) (ii) About 2 mSv.
3.98 (a) (i) about 0.8 cm.
3.99 7.8 μSv.
3.100 4 cm.
3.101 (a) 16×10^{-6} Sv.
 (b) $H = 8 \times 10^{-6}$ Sv.

Uncertainty

1. (a) A. Systematic uncertainty.
  B. Random uncertainty.
  C. Reading uncertainty.
 (c) (i) A. mean = 8.9 V.
   B. mean = 0.52 A.
  (ii) $R = 17.1$ Ω.
2. (a) ±0.1 V.
 (b) ±0.01 mA.
3. (a) mean = 149 μC.
 (b) (i) Random uncertainty = ±8.33 × 10^{-7} C.
  (ii) Percentage uncertainty = 0.56%.
4. (a) (i) % uncertainty in mass = 0.5%.
   % uncertainty in temperature rise = 5%.
   % uncertainty in energy added = 1.2%.
 (b) $c = 4300$ J kg^{-1} °C^{-1} ±5%   or
  $c = 4300$ J kg^{-1} °C^{-1} ±215 J kg^{-1} °C^{-1}.
5. (a) (i) 2.8%.
  (ii) 1%.
 (b) $\lambda = 515 \pm 14$ nm.